DEDICATION

To my dear brother, Yosi z"l,

Without your lifetime of encouragement and guidance, this book could not have been written. I love you and miss you,

Ethan

I highly recommend Dr. Ethan Eisen's scholarly work on the interface of psychology and Judaic concepts. Dr. Eisen astutely compares a wide range of contemporary psychological insights with traditional Jewish thought. He writes with articulate clarity, and reflects in his work a mastery of both Talmudic and psychological concepts. In highlighting the congruence of ancient rabbinic texts with modern psychological knowledge, Dr. Eisen makes an important contribution to both the fields of Judaica and contemporary psychology.

— Dr. Yisrael Levitz
Professor Emeritus, Yeshiva University
Dean, Neve Family Institute, School of Psychotherapy

תפארת גדליה

From the Desk of

RABBI AHRON LOPIANSKY

Rosh HaYeshiva

YGW

Adar 5780

Torah's primary purpose is to address the moral dimension of life, and that is how Chazal's primary meaning should be taken. But being that Torah includes almost every facet of life, there is much knowledge of other aspects of life included in its teachings. It is therefore very enlightening to know the history, physical sciences, etc. that are relevant to different parts of Torah.

Psychology is arguably one of the most closely related disciplines to Torah in general, as both deal with the structure of human nature. While Psychology is highly susceptible to becoming an extension of a personal ideology, there are also many phenomena described that are objective and observable. Being aware of these, will give a person tremendous insight in Chazal's words in many places.

I have known Rabbi Dr. Ethan Eisen, since his high-school days in our Yeshiva. His intelligence, *yiras shamaim*, and extraordinary mentchlichkeit, make him an ideal candidate for producing a work offering insights on so vital a dimension to understanding all aspects of this vital area of Torah.

May he continue to help people with his work as a psychologist, and may he continue to enlighten us with his unique insights.

With heartfelt *bracha,*

Ahron Shraga Lopiansky

ידידי חביבי ר' איתן נ"י

עברתי על הכתבים זעיר פה וזעיר שם כמסת הפנאי נהנתי מהשימוש בכלים
פסיכולוגיים, להוסיף טעם והסבר בדברי רבותינו ז"ל ניכרת חכמה ומלאכה
גדולה ומדוקדקת. מתוך כבוד ויראת הרוממות מול דבריהם ז"ל היות ואינני
מומחה בחכמת הפסיכולוגיה. אינני רואה את עצמי מורשה להביע הסכמה
לגופן של דברים. אבל, בהכירי את טוהר לבך, יושר מדותיך, ויראתך הקודמת
לחכמתך. מובטחני שניתן להגדירך, חבר. שאינו מוציא מתחת ידו דבר שאינו
מתוקן תזכה לעלות מעלה מעלה ולהרבות כבוד שמים המאחל בידידות

מנחם מנדל בלכמן

TALMUD ON THE MIND

Exploring Chazal and
Practical Psychology to Lead a Better Life

Maseches Berachos

Rabbi Dr. Ethan Eisen

KODESH PRESS

Talmud on the Mind: Exploring Chazal and
Practical Psychology to Lead a Better Life (Berachos)
by Ethan Eisen

Paperback Edition ISBN: 978-1-947857-49-0

The Publisher extends its gratitude to Michele Sheer for editing and proofreading this volume.

Published & Distributed Exclusively by

Kodesh Press L.L.C.
New York, NY
www.kodeshpress.com
kodeshpress@gmail.com
sales@kodeshpress.com

Table of Contents

Acknowledgements

This book is a result of many years of learning in yeshivas, universities, and continued self-study. I am forever grateful to my parents, whose dedication allowed me to receive the best education I could have hoped for, and whose value of lifelong study inspires me to learn something new every day. And to my grandparents of blessed memory, whose love and encouragement remains with me.

To Rabbi Ephraim Greenblatt, *zt"l*, whose warmth and wisdom started and sustained me on my path of *limud ha-Torah*. Still to this day, I can close my eyes and put myself back in Rabbi Greenblatt's home. What began as bar mitzvah lessons with Rabbi and Rebbetzin Greenblatt became a second home base for me in Memphis. When I was home for summers or vacation, I would spend hours learning with Rabbi Greenblatt, helping him with various household tasks, listening to him field questions from around the world, or simply speak with him about questions that were on my mind. As I have grown, so has my appreciation of his humble, gentle approach to *harbatzas Torah*.

And to all of my Rabbeim and teachers, who encouraged and challenged me along the way. I am also thankful to Rav Aharon Lopiansky for his thoughtfulness and care in offering feedback on this manuscript. My first opportunity to learn from Rav Lopiansky was in a *chaburah* studying *Alei Shur* as a senior in high school, and even as a youngster, I could appreciate his profound understanding of the human psyche.

When I applied to graduate school, I knew that my relationship with my graduate advisor would be a crucial element of my doctoral experience, but I had no certainty from my various interviews whether my potential advisor would be a good fit. I know how fortunate I am to have had Dr. George Howe as my graduate advisor, whose patience, knowledge, and scholarship helped guide me through graduate school and beyond.

My many years of schooling required commitment from everyone in my family. I am deeply grateful to my wife, Talia, whose joy for life through it all—including eight moves in our first ten years married—makes the journey worthwhile. To my parents and my in-laws, whose moral and material support has made it all possible. And to Aderet, Naama, Nesia, and Gadi, who always keep life exciting.

I am indebted to the various teachers, family members, and friends—Rav Mendel Blachman, Eliezer, Mutti, Elie, among others—who have read parts of the manuscript and provided valuable contributions to the final product. I would often speak with my brother, Yosi, *z"l*, about issues of psychology and *halachah*, and a number of the topics we worked on together are included in this book.

The completion of this book is a testament to the gifts from God that I am blessed to have in my life, and for these I am eternally grateful.

Introduction

The Gemara (*Shabbos* 88b-89a) cites a famous Midrash relating a conversation that occurred between God, the ministering angels, and Moshe, as Moshe ascended Har Sinai to receive the Torah:

> And Rabbi Yehoshua ben Levi said: When Moshe ascended on High to receive the Torah, the ministering angels said before the Holy One, Blessed be He: Master of the Universe, what is one born of a woman doing here among us? The Holy One, Blessed be He, said to them: He came to receive the Torah. The angels said before Him: The Torah is a hidden treasure that was concealed by you 974 generations before the creation of the world, and you seek to give it to flesh and blood?...
>
> The Holy One, Blessed be He, said to Moshe: Provide them with an answer as to why the Torah should be given to the people.... Moshe said before Him: Master of the Universe, the Torah that You are giving me, what is written in it?...
>
> God said to him: "You shall not murder, you shall not commit adultery, you shall not steal." Moshe asked the angels: "Is there jealousy among you, or is there an

evil inclination within you that would render these commandments relevant?" Immediately they agreed with the Holy One, Blessed be He, that He made the right decision to give the Torah to the people, and as it is stated: "God our Lord, how glorious is Your name in all the earth," while "that Your majesty is placed above the heavens" is not written because the angels agreed with God that it is appropriate to give the Torah to the people on earth.

In this passage, the angels question Hashem's decision, so to speak, to give the Torah to human beings. Hashem instructs Moshe to respond, which he does hesitantly. The Gemara records a back-and-forth in the order of the Ten Commandments, and Moshe, for each one, challenges the angels' relevance to the mitzvah. Finally, after asking them, rhetorically, whether jealousy or lust applies to them, the angels agreed with Hashem's decision.

As we see from this Midrash, from the time the Torah was given our Sages recognized and grappled with emotional and psychological questions, and how the *mitzvos* apply to people, each with unique emotional and psychological makeups. Understanding these makeups and the behavioral tendencies that result from them is an essential task of the Chachamim -(or "Chazal," the Sages of the Talmud)-, who are charged with instituting rules to protect the letter and spirit of Torah law. Just as in contemporary psychology, where researchers seek to understand the mechanisms of behavior, Chazal went to great lengths to understand the psychological factors that influence people's behavior. It is exactly this intersection—the writings of our Talmudic Sages with the findings of contemporary psychological science—that this book seeks to explore.

About This Book

The idea for this book originated during my graduate training in psychology, when I began to notice two things. First, I observed that many principles or ideas that we were discussing in class or reading in our textbooks were very similar to concepts I was familiar with from my Torah study. In many cases, these ideas were presented as novel concepts, emerging from sophisticated research designs in the world's top university laboratories. Of course, there is no doubt that many contemporary social scientists are blessed with gifts of genius that help them quantitatively demonstrate mysterious aspects of human psychology and behavior that previously could not be explained. It is equally undeniable that the level of inquiry into specific psychological aspects or mechanisms is more fully fleshed out by modern science than at any previous time in human history. These methods of explanation would be foreign to the Sages of the Talmud. At the same time, the teachings of modern psychology seemed reminiscent of many Jewish teachings. I couldn't help but think about the famous verse in Koheles, "there is nothing new under the sun."

The second observation was that when early writers were introduced into contemporary research or practice, Talmudic wisdom was rarely, if ever, referenced. Introductory psychology courses describe the writings of ancient Greek philosophers, many practitioners cite Buddhist traditions to support their mindfulness training, insights from early Christian writers are sometimes considered, and some textbooks even present ideas from Renaissance-era philosophers. I experienced a certain level of frustration that these courses rarely considered the vast Talmudic and Halachic literature. One can hardly turn a page in the Gemara without some type of insight into human psychology, and this wisdom has largely remained outside the view of contemporary psychological science.

The inverse was also true. As I continued my Torah study, I frequently came across passages in the Talmud or the commentary of Rishonim (medieval Jewish authorities) that had a nuanced reference to a psychological principle that would go largely unaddressed by later commentators. I sometimes wondered if my training in psychology gave me a greater appreciation for the words and depth of the Talmud and its commentators. These thoughts brought to mind the comment of Rabbi Yannai to Rabbi Yochanan, after the latter suggested that a ruling made by Rabbi Yannai was implicit in a well-known Mishnah: "Had I not lifted the earthenware shard for you, would you have discovered the pearl [*marganita*] beneath it?" (*Yevamos* 92b). In other words, without the previous knowledge supplied by Rabbi Yannai, Rabbi Yochanan may not have understood the depth of the Mishnah either. In my case, without my training in psychology, the insights on the pages of the Talmud may have gone undetected.

There are four categories of overlap between Chazal and contemporary science. First, some psychological or behavioral issues are of interest to Chazal, and may have significant halachic ramifications, but are of no interest to modern scientists. For example, the Mishnah rules that on Shabbos, one is liable for the *melachah* (prohibited act on *Shabbos*) of building, *boneh*, even for a tiny act of building (*Shabbos* 102b). The Gemara wonders what the purpose of a small act of building might be. Rabbi Yirmiya provides a suggestion, stating that a poor person "builds" a tiny hole in the ground to protect his few coins. Whereas Chazal were very interested, behaviorally, in how poor people stored their money, I am unaware of modern literature that examines this issue. This question, at least concerning this method of storage, would not be of any interest to modern psychologists or behavioral researchers.

The second category includes topics that modern researchers focus on, in this golden age of social science research with vast diversity of interest, but were not of interest to Chazal, either due to their lack of relevance to topics discussed in the Talmud, or because of technological advances that would not have applied in the past. For example, contemporary researchers have examined the effects of playing the video game Tetris on a wide range of psychological functioning, such as whether it helps with PTSD,[1] or whether it reduces cravings for food,[2] alcohol, drugs, or sex.[3] While the Rabbis may have been interested in how to help someone with PTSD, and were certainly interested in how to approach natural cravings, the

---

1. Holmes, E. A., James, E. L., Coode-Bate, T., & Deeprose, C. (2009). Can playing the computer game "Tetris" reduce the build-up of flashbacks for trauma? A proposal from cognitive science. *PloS one*, 4(1), e4153.
2. Skorka-Brown, J., Andrade, J., & May, J. (2014). Playing 'Tetris' reduces the strength, frequency and vividness of naturally occurring cravings. *Appetite*, 76, 161-165.
3. Skorka-Brown, J., Andrade, J., Whalley, B., & May, J. (2015). Playing Tetris decreases drug and other cravings in real world settings. *Addictive Behaviors*, 51, 165-170.

neuropsychological mechanisms of how video games relate to either was obviously irrelevant to Talmudic discussions.

A third category includes constructs that are identified by Chazal and psychologists, but where neither group provides much elaboration, or the elaboration does not seem to provide much insight into either the Talmudic passage or contemporary scientific understanding. For example, the Gemara (*Berachos* 19b) discusses who among the comforters at a funeral would be exempt from reciting *keriyas Shema* (recitation of the *Shema* passages: *Devarim* 6:4-9, *Devarim* 11:13-21, and *Bamidbar* 15:37-41). It is still the practice that comforters line the road through which the mourner passes extending words of consolation. Rabbi Yehuda rules that those who attend on account of the mourner are exempt from reciting *keriyas Shema*, while those who come for themselves are obligated. Rabbi Shlomi Yitzchaki (Rashi) comments:

"For themselves" — and not out of respect, as they did not come to comfort the mourner, rather out of curiosity [lit., to see the event].

Rashi's understanding is similar to a concept found in a few scientific papers, known as "emotional rubbernecking,"[4] and refers to the idea that people seek to insinuate a closer relationship with the deceased or the family of the deceased than their relationship would call for.

---

4. DeGroot, J. M. (2014). "For whom the bell tolls": Emotional rubbernecking in Facebook memorial groups. *Death Studies*, 38(2), 79-84. This term was found in an earlier non-scientific article: McGowan, K. (2004). Seven Deadly Sentiments. *Psychology Today- New York-*, 37(1), 42-43.

Despite this principle being identified by both Chazal and modern literature, in neither place does the topic receive a great deal of elaboration, and as such, I feel there is not yet enough material to warrant substantial focus.[5]

Finally, the fourth category, and the one discussed in this volume, includes topics that are described both by Chazal and modern scientists, and there is sufficient material to explore what insights each may offer to a certain concept or idea. Sometimes Talmudic or Halachic literature has more to say about a certain topic than contemporary scientific literature; in other instances, modern psychology elaborates more than the Sages did. However, the topics included in this volume include an additional feature. My interest is not just in topics that come up in both worlds; instead, my focus is on how the ideas emerging from one field might allow for a deeper understanding of the other. As a result, I conclude each chapter with a lesson for today that can be gleaned from combining these two sources of knowledge. My goal is to discuss topics that represent the diversity of psychological research, including clinical psychology, neuropsychology, developmental psychology, social psychology, and cognitive psychology. This range of topics displays just a small sliver of the vast knowledge produced by modern research, as well as the diversity of insights presented in the Talmud.

This volume is probably most useful for people familiar with Talmudic texts and concepts, who are also curious about topics in

5. Another similar topic is known as "dark tourism," and relates to the practice of visiting sites of tragic events, like war memorials, terrorist sites, battle fields, prisons, or other locations of human suffering. See the book Lennon, J. J., & Foley, M. (2000). *Dark tourism*. Cengage Learning EMEA.

psychology. The reader need not be an expert in either, although I hope that even those with expertise in either or both of the two fields will find this volume interesting and informative. To make it more accessible to English speakers, quotes from Hebrew sources are translated. Of note, in addition to personally translating some passages, I used a range of sources for translations, including ArtScroll, sefaria.org.il, or Chabad's online resources, depending on the source and language in the excerpt. Also, I briefly define each Hebrew concept the first time it is used.

In selecting the topics to present, I chose to focus on a particular tractate, *Berachos*. Many more areas of overlap exist than I discuss in this volume, and I hope to present them in future works; however, ordering the topics around passages in a specific *masechta* (tractate of the Talmud) can make the topics more accessible, particularly for someone studying or already familiar with this tractate. Finally, I am certain that some arguments that I make in this book may not be convincing to some readers; my intention is not to provide a final word, rather to present ideas that can help the reader appreciate both the wisdom of Chazal and the great contributions of modern psychological research. I hope that the reader benefits as much from reading this volume as I did in preparing it.

Facing Procrastination
Solving Tomorrow's Problem, Today (2a)

אִם כֵּן לָמָה אָמְרוּ חֲכָמִים עַד חֲצוֹת? כְּדֵי לְהַרְחִיק אָדָם מִן הָעֲבֵירָה

[If one really has until dawn to recite keriyas Shema],
why did the Sages say one may only recite it until
midnight? In order to distance a person from sin.

Perhaps there is no better way to appreciate the widespread challenge of procrastination than to observe the dozens of book titles that pop up with an internet search for "overcoming procrastination." Here is a small sample of just a few volumes with that exact phrase in the title:

- *The Complete Idiot's Guide to Overcoming Procrastination,* 2nd Edition
- *The Now Habit: A Strategic Program for Overcoming Procrastination and Enjoying Guilt-Free Play*
- *Overcoming Procrastination: Practice the Now Habit and Guilt-Free Play*
- *Overcoming Procrastination: Or How to Think and Act Rationally in Spite of Life's Inevitable Hassles*
- *Overcoming Procrastination for Teens: A CBT Guide for College-Bound Students*

- *Overcoming Procrastination: 44 Actionable Tips to Take Control of Your Life*

In addition to these books, some of which have multiple editions, there are workbooks and handbooks, funny books and academic books, books for clients and books for clinicians—in short, it is a safe bet that anyone reading this book either does or knows someone who does, struggle with procrastination. One can even read a list of the "95 best productivity books of all time,"[6] all of which promise tips for surefire ways to decrease procrastination and increase productive output. Clearly, despite the enormous interest in breaking patterns of procrastination, it is a habit not easily broken.

Procrastination is a word derived from the Latin *pro-*, meaning "forward," and *crastinus,* meaning "tomorrow." Although scientists have yet to reach a consensus on a single definition of the term,[7] it generally refers to the tendency to delay or postpone completing a task. Why do people procrastinate? Various explanations have been offered ranging from personal characteristics or habits, to features of the tasks being avoided, to explanations based on reward and punishment for completing or not completing the task at hand. Consider the following passage from one of the leading authors on the topic of procrastination:

---

6. Retrieved from https://bookauthority.org/books/best-productivity-books.
7. Steel, P. (2007). The nature of procrastination: A meta-analytic and theoretical review of quintessential self-regulatory failure. *Psychological Bulletin, 133*(1), 65.

22

Procrastination is a mechanism for coping with the anxiety associated with starting or completing any task or decision.[8]

In other words, a person experiences a level of stress when he thinks about having to do something, and procrastination provides him with a way out. Instead of experiencing the anxiety, he can choose to push off the job until later. When he makes that choice he experiences a momentary relief, as the pressure of taking care of the work is no longer weighing on him immediately. It stands to reason that the greater the anxiety about the job—either because of what is at stake, such as at work or school, or because the task is boring or difficult—the greater the relief one experiences when pushing it off until later. In modern times, with shiny and attractive distractions such as phones and computers, the ease with which we can procrastinate makes the challenge all the more likely. In short, procrastination can be seen as a failure of self-regulation, as it happens when we are unable or unwilling to push through our emotions as they gain in intensity, and instead choose the escape-hatch of a distraction or different task, thereby avoiding the difficult emotions altogether.

Of course, procrastination may not be all bad. If it is a tool of cognitive escape that we can employ, it could be helpful to be able to push off some tasks when life becomes overwhelming. Imagine what life would be like if we felt like we had to take care of all of our responsibilities immediately. The pressure would be unbearable! However, when procrastination becomes the norm, it negatively

8. Fiore, N. (2007). *The now habit: A strategic program for overcoming procrastination and enjoying guilt-free play.* New York: J. P. Tarcher/ Penguin.

affects people's productivity, they miss important deadlines, and they suffer regret for having pushed off doing the job until it was too late. As a result, an important question that has been considered by psychologists is: How can we prevent procrastination or its negative outcomes?

Just Do It!

Not surprisingly, Chazal well understood people's inclination toward procrastination. We find many statements that discourage delaying the performance of *mitzvos*—"if a mitzvah comes to your hands, do not allow it to spoil [i.e. do not delay]" *(Mechilta Shemos* 12:7)— as well as other comments encouraging the prompt fulfillment of a mitzvah—"*zerizim* [the vigilant] are early in the performance of *mitzvos*" *(Pesachim* 4a). These statements sound a lot like "Secret #26: Don't Fall Victim to Procrastination" in the book *Get Organized* (page 32)[9]

> A good way to beat procrastination is to 'just do it.' How do you do that? Physically put yourself in a position to start and then sit there for a minute. You'll feel ridiculous if you don't get started.

Of course, Chazal's statements do not add the final clause, that a person will be motivated to start a task because he will feel ridiculous if he doesn't. However, the idea that a person can make an intentional choice to simply do something instead of delaying seems to be the

---

9. Harper, A. (2018). *Get Organized! 52 productivity secrets to master the art of time management.* Author.

theme of the various Rabbinic comments about being vigilant and alacritous.

An instructive example of when the principle of "just do it" is at play relates to Torah study. Researchers have shown that one of the conditions that contributes to a higher likelihood for procrastination is when the task at hand is vague or abstract,[10] which, at least at first glance, describes the mitzvah of Torah study. Consider some of the *halachos* (Jewish laws) pertaining to studying Torah. The Mishnah lists Torah study as a mitzvah that does not have a defined quantity, particularly no maximum (*Peah* 1:1); as such, it is not necessarily clear that person has fulfilled his obligation for Torah study to the fullest extent on any particular day. Additionally, aside from the requirement to review the weekly *parasha* (Torah portion), there are no clear instructions regarding what a person is meant to study; in fact, the Gemara cites Rebbi and Rava as ruling that when selecting a course of study, a person should learn the *sefer* (Jewish book) or topic that piques his interest: "A person should always learn Torah from a place in the Torah that his heart desires" (*Avodah Zarah* 19a).

Torah study contains a number of other elements that make procrastination more likely. Consider the following two statements from the Gemara (*Kiddushin* 30a) related to mastery over Torah.

The Sages taught: The verse states: "And you shall teach them diligently [*ve-shinnantam*]" — that matters of Torah should be sharp and clear in your mouth, so that if a person asks you something, do not stutter in uncertainty and say an uncertain response to him. Rather, answer him immediately.

10. E.g., McCrea, S. M., Liberman, N., Trope, Y., & Sherman, S. J. (2008). Construal level and procrastination. *Psychological Science, 19*(12), 1308-1314.

Rashi explains, "one should review [one's learning] and probe their depth so that if a person asks a question you do not have to stutter, rather you can answer immediately." In other words, a person is required to achieve such mastery that he can respond to questions immediately, without any confusion. On the other hand, as noted by *Shulchan Aruch Ha-Rav* (*Hilchos Talmud Torah* 1:5), a person may reasonably ask how one can possibly master all of Torah that there is to know. After all, the Rabbis teach that Torah's breadth and depth are endless (*Bereishis Rabbah* 10)! Putting these two ideas together, we are left with what may seem like an impossible challenge: we are meant to know everything clearly, but there is no end to what there is to know.

This conundrum—even if not clearly articulated by each student—in addition to the cognitive or intellectual effort required to gain even basic mastery of Torah and Talmudic texts, may have certain psychological effects that contribute to procrastination. As contemporary studies have found,[11] fear of failure, perfectionism, and perceived lack of self-efficacy[12] are all associated with procrastination. One can imagine that someone who approaches Torah study may face these challenges as he realizes the enormity of task of gaining mastery over so much material.

Given all of these potential areas of uncertainty regarding the performance of this mitzvah, as well as the potentially overwhelming

---

11. See Steel (2007) cited above.
12. Self-efficacy is a psychological term related to a person's belief about himself. Generally speaking, it reflects a person's assessment of his own capacity to successfully meet the demands of the world around him. As such, a lack of self-efficacy would mean that a person believes he does not have the tools to succeed.

nature of the expected mastery one is meant to achieve, it is understandable that Chazal would be concerned about people pushing off studying by engaging in other activities, particularly the pursuit of financial gains, as Rabbi Moshe ben Maimon (Rambam) describes:

> Perhaps, one will say: "[I will interrupt my studies] until after I gather money, and then I will return and study, [I will interrupt my studies] until after I buy what I need, and then, when I can divert my attention from my business, I will return and study." If you consider such thoughts, you will never merit the crown of Torah (*Hilchos Talmud Torah* 3:7).

Rambam is depicting how a person may justify pushing off the study of Torah in pursuit of prosperity. Although he does not explicitly describe that Torah study is particularly vulnerable to procrastination, a careful examination points in this direction. Rambam does not make this comment regarding other *mitzvos*, such as saying "perhaps one will say I will pray once I earn enough money," or "I will honor my parents once I make money," or "I will sit in the *sukkah* once I have enough money." As Rambam describes, gaining mastery over Torah requires herculean effort, as he puts eloquently several *halachos* later:

> The words of Torah will not be permanently acquired by a person who applies himself feebly [to obtain] them, and not by those who study amid pleasure and [an abundance] of food and drink. Rather, one must give up his life for them,

constantly straining his body to the point of discomfort, without granting sleep to his eyes or slumber to his eyelids (*Talmud Torah* 3:12).

As noted above, psychologically speaking it is exactly this feature of Torah study that may make it more likely for someone to avoid starting. He may feel overwhelmed by the commitment required to achieve success, and choose to not even try for fear of failure, perfectionism, or low self-efficacy. Rambam, based on *Pirkei Avos*, offers the following "just do it" recommendation for combatting this problem:

Rather, make your work secondary, and your Torah study a fixed matter. Do not say: "When I have free time, I will study," for perhaps you will never have free time (*Talmud Torah* 3:7).

In other words, make an intentful, conscious decision to combat the urge to avoid Torah study, and just do it!

Do It Sooner...

Despite the numerous comments by Chazal encouraging potential procrastinators to "just do it," it is clear that encouragement to do things early is not always sufficient. So it is fitting that in the Talmud's opening Mishnah, Chazal offer an additional method to reducing procrastination, namely the imposition of costly, albeit artificial, deadlines (*Berachos* 2a).

[Rabban Gamliel said] wherever the Sages say until midnight, the precept may be performed until the dawn comes up...Why then did the Sages say "until midnight"? In order to keep a man far from transgression.

Rashi explains:

[Regarding] *keriyas Shema* [they said this] in order to urge [*le-zarez*] a person so that he will not say, "I still have more time," and as a result the daybreak will come and he will have missed the time [to perform the mitzvah].

A few important ideas emerge from this Mishnah and Rashi's commentary. First, according to Rashi, it was the need to counter the tendency for a person to procrastinate, namely to postpone the fulfillment of the mitzvah of *keriyas Shema*, that compelled Chazal to institute a new deadline for completing this requirement. Second, there is no indication that Chazal thought that procrastination was necessarily a reaction to anxiety or fear about starting or completing a task, as the more straightforward interpretation of Rashi is that he is describing a deficit in prioritizing the performance of a mitzvah[13]; instead of stopping his current activity, this person decides that he prefers to continue what he's doing and recite *keriyas Shema* later, as he still has plenty of time.

Finally, in this instance, Chazal's method for solving the problem of procrastination is to set a new deadline for completing this requirement. The effectiveness of this strategy, while it has been

---

13. See also Rashi, *Shabbos* 34a, s.v. *im chasheicha*.

debated among various writers on the topic of procrastination, has been confirmed in recent psychological literature. In one study of college students, researchers found that those who had artificial deadlines made fewer errors in their work and were more likely to complete their tasks on time.[14]

It is worth considering why moving a deadline up may be helpful. One likely possibility, that on its face seems to run counter to the idea that procrastination is a fear- or anxiety- avoidance behavior, is that increased anxiety or pressure actually *motivates* a person to act. Although for some people rising emotional intensity can cause psychological paralysis, for most people once the deadline is imminent, we are more focused and motivated to start and complete the job. This idea is also consistent with the long-observed psychological principle that the greater the temporal distance of an event, the less that event will motivate one's current behavior;[15] by moving the timeline forward for reciting *keriyas Shema*, Chazal have increased the salience and pressure of the deadline in a person's mind, and reduced the likelihood of missing the time due to procrastination.

...Or Else!

What happens if the "just do it" or "do it sooner" approaches don't work? Some authors have suggested looking to extrinsic motivators

14. Ariely, D., & Wertenbroch, K. (2002). Procrastination, deadlines, and performance: Self-control by precommitment. *Psychological Science*, 13(3), 219-224.

15. E.g., Peetz, J., Wilson, A. E., & Strahan, E. J. (2009). So far away: The role of subjective temporal distance to future goals in motivation and behavior. *Social Cognition*, 27(4), 475-495.

(i.e., reward and punishment) to help ensure that jobs get done. Does penalizing procrastination help prevent procrastination? While this carrot-and-stick approach seems intuitive, and may be effective in some instances,[16] Chazal did not necessarily hold a person liable if procrastination was partially responsible for a missed deadline. Take, for example, what some Acharonim (post-medieval recent halachic authorities) point to as an apparent discrepancy in the rulings of *Shulchan Aruch*. In one place, regarding making up missed *tefillos* (prayers),[17] *Shulchan Aruch* rules:

> Someone who did not pray while he still had time because he thought that he would have enough time after he finishes whatever he is involved with, and at the end the time for *tefillah* passed... he is considered 'compelled' (*ahnus*), and may make up the *tefillah* (*Orach Chaim* 108:8).

According to this *halachah* (Jewish law), it appears that a person is not penalized for postponing praying due to his involvement in some other activity. However, regarding fulfilling an oath Rabbi Moshe Isserles (Rema) presents opposing viewpoints

> If someone took an oath to do a specified thing within a year... he should do it immediately lest he forget later and not do it, and he will have transgressed his oath. But if he

---

16. See Steel (2007) for a discussion.
17. The basic *halachah* is that a person who misses a *tefillah* purposefully may not make it up, but if missing the *tefillah* was not purposeful he may make it up by reciting a second *Amidah* in the following prayer service.

did not do it immediately because he said 'I still have time to do it' and he forgot or an *oness* (unforeseen event) occurred later and he did not do it, some authorities say that this is considered "being compelled" (*ahnus*), while others say it is not considered "being compelled" (*Yoreh De'ah* 232:12).

The *Magen Avraham*'s approach[18] is commonly cited explanation for why in regard to *tefillah Shulchan Aruch* clearly accepts one position that an *oness* on the last day is considered an *oness* and one is not penalized for delaying, while in regard to oaths Rema also presents the minority view that it is not considered an *oness*. He suggests that regarding oaths, about which we are generally very concerned about their violations, there may be reason to be more stringent.[19] According to this approach, it appears that Chazal, in general, were reluctant to hold a person liable for procrastination, but the *poskim* (modern-day authorities in *halachah*) were willing to penalize someone in instances that the consequences of missing the deadline are considered especially serious.

Why would Chazal be hesitant to penalize someone for procrastination? After all, if extrinsic motivators work to reduce procrastination, what would be the drawback? Perhaps the following passage provides some insight:[20]

---

18. *Orach Chaim* 108, note 11; see also *Machatzis HaShekel*, ad loc.
19. See Rambam, *Hilchos Sanhedrin* 7:10 Frankel edition *Sefer Ha-Mafte'ach* for many more Acharonim who discuss this *machlokes*.
20. Ludwig, P., & Schicker, A. (2018). *The end of procrastination: How to stop postponing and live a fulfilled life*. New York: St. Martins Griffin.

The imaginary stick hanging over us often makes us despise what we have to do. This stick may come in the form of mortgage payments that prevent people from quitting the jobs they loathe, it might be parents picking out hobbies or college majors and forcing them on their children, or it could be the boss at work who gives his subordinates assignments without explaining why. Antipathy is a natural outcome of extrinsic stimuli and often causes procrastination to grow.

Imagine if the motivation for hurrying-up and davening was a penalty laid down by Chazal—would this make a person more likely to pray with *kavanah* (focus) or less likely? The case seems to be describing a person who wants to daven, is interested in praying, just is distracted by something else. If we tell him that his punishment is that he is not allowed to make up the prayer—that he should have been more organized about his time management to begin with—we are taking what was something he wanted to do, and turning it into a burden. Perhaps for this reason *Shulchan Aruch* insisted that the case of a procrastinator be considered a case of *oness*, thereby allowing him to make up the *tefillah*, even if we lose the potential gain of a penalizing extrinsic motivator. The opposite may be true as it relates to taking an oath. Chazal regarded oathtaking as negative (*Shulchan Aruch Yoreh De'ah 203:1*), and any measure that reduces the likelihood of an oath would be encouraged. As such, if punishing a person for not fulfilling his oath would mean he begins to despise to the act of oathtaking, that would be a desirable outcome.

If this approach is correct, we can learn a valuable lesson in regard to combatting procrastination and other challenges in life:

while a certain approach may help in the short-term, if the long-term effects run counter to our desired goal, it may be best to prioritize the long-term goals over the short-term results.

Lesson for Today

Among the most common difficulties articulated by clients in my practice, particularly for those in academic settings, is trouble starting or completing tasks, and pushing off important items until the last minute. This tendency to push off necessary work may be related to difficulty with attention, such as Attention Deficit Hyperactivity Disorder; challenges managing anxiety or other disruptive or distracting emotional states; or various life-circumstances that make starting or completing tasks more difficult. The impact of this procrastination is real, as people sometimes produce work of lesser quality, fail to get things done by deadlines, or experience high levels of stress and anxiety as the deadline for completion approaches. And as many clients discover, whatever the cause or causes, and whatever the impact, procrastination is a hard habit to break, and hundreds, or probably thousands, of books, chapters, articles, and personal communications have been devoted to conquering this ubiquitous challenge. As such, it is very fitting that Chazal address the issue of procrastination on the opening page of the Talmud, and, in some ways, the diversity of the Rabbinic comments highlights the uniqueness of each person's procrastination—no one strategy will work every time for every person, and for that reason a variety of strategies are necessary to have in one's repertoire to combat the inclination to procrastinate the performance of commandments or other necessary tasks.

Perhaps before settling on a set of strategies for combatting procrastination, the most important step comes before the circumstances that lead to procrastinating. Instead of searching for a solution in the midst of panic, I often work with people to be mindful of what situations are upcoming in which they may be likely to procrastinate. This preceding awareness provides the opportunity to come up with a plan before the intensity builds to complete the necessary task, and also allows for the individual to consider, with a clearer head, which strategies are likely to be the most effective. We share the challenges of procrastination with generations before us spanning thousands of years, and developing skills for managing it—and taking guidance from the Sages—can help us live more productive and meaningful lives as *ovdei Hashem* (servants of God).

Who Needs Sleep?
King David and the Circadian Rhythm (3b)

רַבִּי זֵירָא אָמַר: מֹשֶׁה לְעוֹלָם הֲוָה יָדַע,

וְדָוִד נָמֵי הֲוָה יָדַע, וְכֵיוָן דְּדָוִד הֲוָה יָדַע כִּנּוֹר לָמָה לֵיהּ? לְאִתְּעוֹרֵי מִשֵּׁנְתֵּיהּ

If David knew, then why did he need the harp?
The Gemara answers: He needed the harp to wake him from his sleep.

In 2018, British sailor Alex Thomson was nearing the finish line with a 15-hour lead over his closest competitor in the Route de Rhum, a 3,542-nautical mile solo transatlantic sailboat race. In addition to being a skilled sailor who holds the record for the fastest Briton to sail solo around the world, Thomson is well-known for a different type of physical feat: he only sleeps in short naps, roughly 20-30 minutes, every two hours: "I trained myself to sleep for 20 minutes every two hours. It's the only way to sail around the world if you're on your own."[21] Practicing this sleep regimen for the Route de Rhum, Thomson was set to win by a longshot, and he was ready for one more nap just a few hours from the finish of the race. He set his alarm, as well as his shockwave watch as a backup, and closed his

21. Retrieved from https://www.dailymail.co.uk/health/article-2729413/Can-sleeping-two-hours-day-make-productive-Or-make-grumpy-zombie-Our-brave-man-stripey-pyjamas-test.html.

eyes for a rest. As it happened, he did not wake up from the alarm, the shockwave watches batteries were not sufficiently charged, and he awoke to his boat crashing against the rocks on the wrong shore of the race's terminal island: "I expected to arrive in Guadeloupe today, not hit it."[22]

Many people, like Thomson, try to manipulate their sleep to accommodate the pressures felt in other aspects of their lives. As we try to balance life's many demands, including professional responsibilities, family life, spiritual pursuits, and other needs, sleep schedules are often shifted or shortened, often with mixed results. On the one hand, more time awake means that one can be more productive, take care of more things, and fit more activity into any given day. On the other hand, sleep deprivation leads to cognitive, emotional, and health disturbances, as the reporter from the *Daily Mail*, Tom Mitchelson, found when he tried to model his sleep schedule after Thomson's:[23]

I've ceased to function properly and need people with me for my safety. My inability to nap has given me a real sympathy for insomniacs. It's like torture. I go shopping, but get so confused while buying milk, I have to ask the shop assistant to talk me through my change. Even then, I can barely understand her explanation. I stare at the coins, unsure as to their value. I feel vulnerable and as if my brain

22. Retrieved from https://www.bbc.com/sport/sailing/46238013.
23. Retrieved from https://www.dailymail.co.uk/health/article-2729413/Can-sleeping-two-hours-day-make-productive-Or-make-grumpy-zombie-Our-brave-man-stripey-pyjamas-test.html.

is slowly dying. It's what I imagine victims of dementia feel like. Certainty that you know what is going on around you, then a sudden disintegration of that certainty, which leaves you feeling vulnerable.

Thomson and Mitchelson were each trying to implement what is known as the "Uberman," an extreme version of a type of sleep pattern known as "polyphasic sleep." As opposed to most people who obtain their hours of sleep in one chunk—monophasic sleep—their type of sleep schedule involves multiple smaller chunks of sleep spread throughout the day; indeed, according to some halachic sources, polyphasic sleep with short sleep intervals may be preferred if a person is healthy enough to sustain such a schedule.[24]

How King David Slept

Although the first person specified by the Torah who adjusted or limited his sleep was Yaakov as he tended to Lavan's herds (*Bereishis* 31:40), in the Talmud, it is King David whose sleep patterns draw the most interest. In addition to the reference to possible polyphasic sleep cycles,[25] *Sefer Tehillim* (Book of Psalms) is full of King David's personal descriptions of how life circumstances affected his sleep quantity and quality. However, as I hope to show, contemporary

---

24. See commentators on *Sukkah* 26b, regarding the sleeping pattern of some Amoraim, based on the tradition of King David's sleeping pattern. See also *Tur/Shulchan Aruch* 231, as well as *Aruch Ha-Shulchan* 231 for a more focused examination.
25. For a survey of various halachic issues related to sleep, see Rabbi Aryeh Leibowitz's review: download.yutorah.org/2009/1109/735393.pdf.

research on sleep cycles may provide a deeper understanding of a specific sleeping pattern of King David described in the Talmud.

The Gemara records a disagreement about King David's nocturnal sleeping habits (*Berachos* 3b). According to Rabbi Zeira, David would doze until midnight, and then awaken after midnight; Rav Ashi held that David would learn Torah until midnight, and then sing Hashem's praises after midnight. The Gemara then presents the following discussion:

> But did David know the exact time of midnight? Even Moshe Rabbeinu did not know it![26]... David had a sign. For so said Rav Aha bar Bizna in the name of Rabbi Shimon Hasida: A harp was hanging above David's bed. As soon as midnight arrived, a North wind came and blew upon it and it played of itself. He arose immediately and studied the Torah till the break of dawn....
>
> Rabbi Zeira says: Moshe certainly knew and David, too, knew [the exact time of midnight]. Since David knew, why did he need the harp? That he might wake from his sleep.[27]

According to Rabbi Zeira, how did Moshe and David know? Regarding Moshe, for whom the knowledge of midnight was only necessary for that single day, it is possible that Hashem related to him a prophecy or astronomical sign through which he could discern

26. The Gemara refers to the final plague, which Moshe proclaims will occur "around midnight."

27. This is consistent with a previous opinion of Rabbi Zeira that David lightly dozed the first half of the night, and thus required some stimulation to help him arise.

the exact time of midnight. But for David, the Gemara implies he arose daily at this time. It seems unlikely that he would rely on astronomical indications of midnight: first, how could he do this daily, even on cloudy days; and second, one opinion in the Gemara states that he was dozing until this point, so he would certainly be unable to look up at the heavens!

Although none of the commentators explain how, according to Rabbi Zeira, King David knew the exact time of midnight, the most reasonable explanation seems to be that David had entrained himself to be in sync with a midnight wakeup; based on modern science, we may suggest that he made use of his *circadian rhythm* to successfully entrain his body to awake at a specific, identical time each day. The circadian rhythm is something of an internal clock, and refers to "variations in physiology and behavior that persist with a cycle length close to 24 hours even in the absence of periodic environmental stimuli" (Duffy & Czeisler, 2009, p. 2); the sleep-wake cycle is one of these functions. Although many people may not be actively aware of the influence of the circadian rhythm on their functioning, most people have experienced jetlag, which is a result of one's circadian clock being out of sync with one's time-zone; it may take a number of days for the body to adjust to a new 24-hour cycle.

Although a comprehensive discussion of the various brain-structures thought to contribute to different aspects of the circadian rhythms in humans, the primary area of brain responsible for keeping the circadian rhythm on pace is known as the suprachiasmic nucleus (SCN). One interesting feature of the SCN is that exposure to light is largely responsible for resetting the cycle; as a result, when overcoming jetlag, exposing oneself to sunlight is often recommended as an effective, safe, and non-pharmaceutical option to recalibrate one's circadian rhythm.[28] Additionally, and relevant to the passage about King David, exposure to light can reset the circadian clock to a 24-hour cycle, even while the circadian cycle in any particular person may be slightly longer or shorter than 24-hours if left undisturbed. The basic process involved in this light-based reset is that SCN receives signals from cells in the retina that are sensitive to light, which triggers a response to reset the circadian cycle.

Over the years, scientists have tried to determine how different types or intensities of light affect the circadian rhythm. In one fascinating study,[29] researchers studied whether different light intensities could entrain or reset the circadian cycle at varying intervals: 24 hours, 23.5 hours, 24.5 hours, etc. Among their various findings, they reported that "the unanticipated finding that these human subjects remained entrained to the 24.0-h day in candlelight is remarkable given that this illuminance level is less than one-thousandth of the intensity once thought to be necessary for entrainment" (p. 14031). Additionally, the ability of candlelight to reset the circadian was not found at other intervals, such as 23.5 or 24.5 hours.

---

28. E.g., Parry, B. L. (2002). Jet lag: Minimizing its effects with critically timed bright light and melatonin administration. *Journal of Molecular Microbiology and Biotechnology*, 4(5), 463-466.

29. Wright, K. P., Hughes, R. J., Kronauer, R. E., Dijk, D. J., & Czeisler, C. A. (2001). Intrinsic near-24-h pacemaker period determines limits of circadian entrainment to a weak synchronizer in humans. *Proceedings of the National Academy of Sciences*, 98(24), 14027-14032.

Based on this study, we can suggest a method by which King David trained his body to know the exact time of midnight each day. Imagine for a moment what his experience was as the harp played at midnight to awake him. As he opened his eyes in a dark room, filled with the sound of the harp, he immediately called for a servant to light a flame so that he may commence his study of Torah. As he settled down at the table to learn, the candle is just beside him, illuminating the parchment as he reads. Perhaps in addition to simply being an aid to his learning, it seems possible that this candlelight may also have reset his circadian cycle for a 24-hour cycle from midnight to midnight, allowing him to repeat this cycle the following night as well, at the same time. After a short period of time, David may have come to notice physiological patterns that clued him in to the time of day or night.

This answer may be especially compelling according to Rabbi Moshe Feinstein's implication that *chatzos* (halachic midnight/midday) should be seen as a fixed time—i.e., always exactly 24 hours apart, and the length of the days/nights are what shift around it;[30] it would have been necessary for King David to entrain himself to a rhythm of exactly 24-hours to know exactly the time of *chatzos*, which also would have helped him be ready to arise quickly to the sound of his harp. If this approach is true,[31] it would also suggest that King David figured out how to use dim candlelight to reset his circadian rhythm thousands of years before its discovery by

30. *Igros Moshe, Orach Chaim* 2:20.
31. It is clearly not the opinion of Rabbi Noson in the Talmud Yerushalmi (*Berachos* 1:1) who states that King David would sometimes get up at midnight, and sometimes two hours prior to midnight).

scientists. Additionally, if this is interpretation is correct, it would not be the only place that Chazal record that King David's body was in tune with spiritual pursuits. The Midrash comments, based on *Tehillim* 119:59, that though King David had plans to go to various places, out of habit or desire for closeness to Hashem, his legs would carry him to houses of prayer and study (*Vayikra Rabbah* 35:1).

Lessons for Today

Although the Gemara clearly has a positive view of King David's supreme effort to limit his physical needs in pursuit of lofty spiritual goals, it is also clear that the *poskim* do not expect most people to achieve, or even attempt, his physical feats; as demonstrated by the contrast between Alex Thomson and Tom Mitchelson, extreme sleeping habits are certainly not for everyone. Nevertheless, from a psychological perspective, we can learn some valuable lessons from King David's example.

Perhaps most importantly, the Gemara's and commentators' interest in sleep highlights that sleep is an essential need of human beings.[32] Although this may seem like an obvious idea, very often sleep is something of an afterthought for people as they prioritize the needs of the day. I am reminded of an experience from years ago, sitting around a Shabbos table with a group of young professionals, many of whom were small business owners, and others who were employees in larger businesses or organizations. A discussion began about people's use of sleeping techniques and aids, with many of the people speaking about how they use some type of medication to help them sleep. I was intrigued by how casually everyone seemed

---

32. For example, see Rashi *Sukkah* 26a, s.v. *de-paris sudra alayhu.*

to be describing their use of sleeping pills, so I posed a question to the people around the table: "If you had to guess, what percentage of working people use sleeping pills regularly?" One of the more vocal guests at the table responded, "I'd say around 70%." Most others at the table appeared to be nodding approvingly. I am doubtful that the rate of usage is that high, as some recent studies seem to place the number across the USA population at around 4%;[33] however, the perception that difficulty sleeping is that common, and that the preferred solution is a medical one, surprised me a great deal. These passages in Talmudic literature, and the fact that the more extreme types of sleep schedules are not codified in *halachah*, remind us that sleep is an essential part of life, and that considering our needs for sleep is necessary and a legitimate halachic value.

On the other hand, King David provides a crucial perspective regarding choices we can make to bring our physical needs in line with spiritual pursuits. Many of us develop beliefs over time about what we "need" to function, including about sleep. For example, a colleague I once worked with commented that without her ten hours of sleep, she really can't be functional the following day. Of course, it may be true that some people need ten hours of sleep to be able to function well. However, King David is teaching us an important lesson that we must balance our physical needs with the pursuit of our loftier values. Just as Alex Thomson experimented with his sleeping pattern in pursuit of greater achievement in the world of sailing, we may be able to achieve greater fulfillment in our lives by gaining more understanding of our physical needs and limitations—

---

33. Retrieved from https://www.livescience.com/39278-americans-use-prescription-sleeping-pills.html.

and where we can push the limits. Maybe that means staying up an extra twenty minutes to learn something at the end of the day; maybe one spouse, before running off to work, can wake up a little earlier and make lunches so the morning is a little bit easier for the rest of the family; maybe it means taking a shorter nap on Shabbos so that one can play a game with his children, have a *chavrusa*, or go on a walk with one's family. Perhaps it is best summarized by the following passage in *Aruch Ha-Shulchan* (*Orach Chaim* 231:1-4), which emphasizes one's values should be focused on *avodas Hashem* [the service of God] in fulfilling one's various physical needs:

> It is certain regarding [sleep] that it depends on the individual... as we have even seen great scholars who would sleep for an hour or two during the daytime, as this was necessary for them according to their energy levels and daily routines....
>
> [However], according to the *Beis Yosef* [who writes that a person may not sleep more than a very short period during the day], this is only for something whose health is good and can suffice with very little sleep....
>
> And even with little amount of sleep, a person's intent should not be simply for the physical benefit; instead he should have intent to strengthen himself for service of Hashem, such as to learn Torah or perform *mitzvos*. And even for someone who is working to support his family through labor or business who requires rest during the day in order to toil in his work, this is also permitted...with the intent that this rest is *l'sheim Shamayim* [for God's sake].

The more we are able to bring our physical needs and practices in line with our greater values in life, the more fulfillment we can have in all aspects of our lives. However, according to the suggestion of this chapter, the lesson from King David is even greater. Not only are we able to raise the importance of our physical needs by infusing them with spiritual ideals, the opposite can also be true. By gaining a better understanding of our physical processes and needs, we can make our spiritual life more fulfilling as well. Indeed, King David may have used an understanding of his natural body clock, and how to regulate it, to allow him to achieve the loftiest of spiritual heights. Similarly, we may see great gains in our values and spirituality if we develop a deeper and more sensitive understanding of our physical bodies and functions.

Skin Deep Emotions

Physiological Expression of Shame and Fear (6b)

נוֹחַ לוֹ לְאָדָם שֶׁיַּפִּיל עַצְמוֹ לְתוֹךְ כִּבְשָׁן הָאֵשׁ וְאַל יַלְבִּין פְּנֵי חֲבֵרוֹ בָּרַבִּים

"It is better for a man that he should cast himself into a fiery furnace rather than that he should put his fellow to shame in public"
(Berachos 43b; Bava Metzia 59a; Sotah 10b)

In 2004, the American Ninth Circuit Court of Appeals upheld a lower court's ruling in a case referred to as *U.S. v. Gementera*. The facts of the case involved a young adult who was convicted of stealing mail, and the judge presiding over the case sentenced the offender to two months incarceration, and three years of supervised release, involving 100 hours of community service. In an unusual move, one of the conditions of the supervised release was the requirement for the offender to stand in front of a post-office with a placard containing the following text: "I stole mail. This is my punishment."[34]

Part of the argument put forth by the sentencing judge explaining

---

34. Ziel, P. (2005). Eighteenth century public humiliation penalties in twenty-first century America: The "shameful" return of" scarlet letter" punishments in *US v. Gementera. Brigham Young University Journal of Public Law*, 19(2), 499-522.

the use of public humiliation was that "such an experience should have a specific rehabilitative effect on defendant that could not be accomplished by other means." In other words, the experience of humiliation was meant to encourage the offender to appreciate the gravity of his crime, and choose to abandon criminal activity for the future. Notably, not all American legal scholars support the idea of using humiliation as a form of rehabilitation or punishment.

The legal debate seems to revolve around the question of whether humiliation would be effective in deterrence or rehabilitation. Both sides seem to agree that if rehabilitation were not achieved, simply using humiliation as a punishment would be too severe. Neither side in this case seemed to offer an explanation for *why* public humiliation would be considered such a strong punishment; of course, it is unpleasant, but there are many unpleasant things that are used as punishments, and we typically do not assess whether these unpleasant experiences necessarily have a rehabilitative effect. There seems to be something unique to the experience of humiliation that separates its experience from other types of unpleasant or punishing conditions. Indeed, the Gemara implies that in some ways, it is specifically the shame, not the physical pain, that is the fulfillment of Biblical punishment of lashes (*Makkos* 22-23). This sentiment is also expressed in the Yom Kippur liturgy recited after the *Ma'ariv* (evening prayer) service:[35] "Note our embarrassment and reckon it as retribution for iniquity." A careful read of one passage in the Gemara, in light of some insights from psychological science, may help provide a better understanding of one aspect of humiliation's

---

35. *Selichah* with the refrain *salachti*.

punishing nature,[36] and why it may be regarded differently than other types of punishment.

Understanding Humiliation

For the most part, the debate surrounding *U.S. v. Gementera* is concerned with the post-humiliation effects; will the offender reconsider his ways as a result of experiencing the humiliation, as the judge asserted optimistically? Or as others might argue, will the offender instead become "withdrawn, depressed, or even angry," or perhaps even "wear their 'Scarlet Letter' as a badge of honor"? Others have argued that those who suffer humiliation may turn to

---

36. I am not addressing whether *halachah* would allow for or recommend such a punishment, although it may be a debate among the poskim. There is a general principle that the Rabbinic leaders in a community may engage in extra-legal punishment as they see fit, known at *onshim she-lo min ha-din*. However, it may be that use of humiliation is not universally agreed upon. The Gemara (*Megillah* 25b) comments that "Rav Ashi said: One whose reputation is tarnished [i.e., he is known as a philanderer], it is permitted to humiliate him." At first glance, the context of this statement is that a person generally may not mock others; the Gemara then discusses some exceptions, such as when referring to idols or idol worshipers. However, this passage seems to be the source of Rambam's ruling (*Hilchos Sanhedrin* 24:5) that the courts may disparage or humiliate others as part of the practice of *onshim she-lo min ha-din*. Although *Tur* (*Choshen Mishpat* 2) cites Rambam's language, *Shulchan Aruch* does not include this clause. For several examples of when humiliation was used practically in the Jewish community, see Rashi, T., & Rosenberg, H. (2017). *Shaming in Judaism: Past, present, future. Journal of Religion and Society*, v.19.

revenge as a way of coping with lingering feelings of humiliation. But to really understand humiliation and its punishing nature, it is necessary to consider the peri-event impact, i.e., what is happening as the embarrassing event is going on.

Although humiliation has not received the same level of attention by researchers as have other emotions, several features have emerged from empirical studies.[37] The experience of humiliation is connected to feeling powerless, dishonored, and belittled, which also likely have a deleterious effect on a person's self-esteem. As one might expect, emotions of disappointment, anger, and shame are also associated with humiliation. For many people, each of these emotions can be sources of discomfort or distress, and may be punishing experiences in their own right.

In addition to the emotional impact central to a humiliating event, one may also experience a range of cognitive effects that increase the unpleasantness and terror. For example, on a cognitive level, despite a general assumption in the literature that humiliation is basically synonymous with shame, contemporary researchers have argued that these two similar emotions actually have a number of critical differences. One main difference is that regarding the experience of shame, people tend to hold themselves responsible for the prompting circumstances, while regarding humiliation, people tend to place the onus of responsibility on someone else. As such, people who suffer humiliation may experience a greater sense of unfairness, as they believe they did not deserve the experience. A victim of humiliation may also have self-critical thoughts of looking foolish or thoughts of vulnerability.

---

37. Elshout, M., Nelissen, R. M., & van Beest, I. (2017). Conceptualizing humiliation. *Cognition and Emotion*, 31(8), 1581-1594.

The Physiology of Humiliation

Finally, humiliation takes a physical toll on the victim through physiological changes. Even though contemporary researchers have not focused specifically on the physiological effects of humiliation, the Gemara (*Berachos* 6b) provides a fascinating insight into the nature of how the physiological responses to humiliation are punishing:

> One of the Sages said to Rav Beivai bar Abaye... What is the meaning of the verse: "When vileness is exalted [*kerum*] among the sons of men"?... Rabbi Yochanan and Rabbi Elazar, both said: Once a person needs the help of others [Rashi: and loses dignity in their eyes], his face changes and becomes like a *kerum*, as it is stated: "When vileness [*kerum*] is exalted among the sons of men." What is *kerum*? When Rav Dimi came to Babylonia from the land of Israel he said: There is a bird in the cities by the sea called *kerum* and when the sun rises, the bird changes several colors.

The Gemara continues with a further description of the effects of this reaction to feeling inferior to others, thereby being disparaged in the public eye:

> Rav Ammi and Rav Assi both say: it is as if he was punished with two punishments: Fire and water. As it is stated: "You have caused men to ride over our heads; we have gone through fire and water."

As Rabbi Shmuel Eidels (Maharsha) explains, when a person is confronted with public shame or humiliation—and public could mean in the presence of just a single other person—two distinct reactions are likely, and are characterized by "fire" and "water": he may blush, i.e. become red in the face; or he may become pale-faced, losing the color that is typically present. Contemporary research elaborates on each of these reactions to offer a deeper understanding of the physiological experience described by the Gemara.

Blushing

Blushing, as most are familiar, "involves the reddening of one's face, ear, neck, and upper chest, and is produced by increases in blood volume in the subcutaneous surface capillaries in those regions (p. 256)."[38] At least as far back as 1839,[39] medical, biological, and psychological researchers have been interested in the blushing reaction displayed by people in an apparent response to some emotional experience. More recently, researchers have identified several categories of circumstances that often elicit blushing, although not all of them immediately appear to be related to humiliation, including threats to public identity, positive attention, scrutiny, and accusations of blushing.[40] The first—threats to public identity—is what Darwin thought was at the root of all cases of

---

38. Keltner, D., & Buswell, B. N. (1997). Embarrassment: Its distinct form and appeasement functions. *Psychological Bulletin*, 122(3), 250-270.

39. Burgess, T. H. (1839). *The physiology or mechanism of blushing.* Churchill.

40. Leary, M. R., Britt, T. W., Cutlip, W. D., & Templeton, J. L. (1992). Social blushing. *Psychological Bulletin, 112*(3), 446-460.

social blushing, as he wrote: "blushing... depends in all cases on the same principle; this principle being a sensitive regard for the opinion, more particularly for the depreciation of others." In other words, when a circumstance arises that leads a person to feel that his public standing has been diminished—often described through the emotions of embarrassment or shame—blushing is a common physiological response.

This cause of blushing, the type associated with the threat to public identity, seems to be the one referred to in our Gemara, as the person being described appears to be self-sufficient and then becomes dependent on others for support. However, the Gemara seems to be extending this idea further: not only does humiliation lead to blushing, this physiological response is itself a penalty. According to this reading, blushing is not only a sign of the contemporaneous mistreatment, it is also a portion of punishment that one is receiving. The red face and increased skin-temperature[41] are comparable to the experience of being burned, and as such it is considered a punishment by fire.

Pale Face

In contrast to blushing that is compared to fire, the pale-face reaction is compared to punishment by water. The phenomenon of the pale-face has drawn less interest by researchers, but it seems to be related to different emotions than the blush. Some of the interest in recent years has emerged from the field of video graphics, as artists try to accurately

---

41. E.g., Shearn, D., Bergman, E., Hill, K., Abel, A., & Hinds, L. (1990). Facial coloration and temperature responses in blushing. *Psychophysiology, 27*(6), 687-693.

simulate the facial features of various emotions.[42] Pale complexion is associated with emotions such as fear, panic, and apprehension, but not typically with embarrassment and shame. In line with a reaction to something fearful, the pale-face response may be due to the activation of the sympathetic nervous system (i.e., fight or flight response);[43] this physiological system causes a constriction of blood flow to parts of the body that are not essential for fight or flight, such as the cheeks and face, leading to a loss of color and pale complexion.

At first glance, the contemporary findings seem to be at odds with the understanding of our Gemara. Based on most interpretations of our Gemara, both the red- and pale-face phenomena are seen in response to something that causes *bushah*, shame or embarrassment; however, modern research only connects blushing in the face to shame, and pale-face is related to panic or fear. It is possible that Chazal and contemporary science are at odds regarding what types of events may precipitate the pale-face response. However, a closer look indicates that there may be agreement in this case, based on a profound understanding of the way emotions are experienced and expressed.

The Mishnah in *Pirkei Avos* (3:11) counts someone who publicly humiliates another (lit., "causes another's face to go white") as forfeiting his share in the World to Come. Using the scientific language of his time, Rav Bartenura explains:

---

42. Jung, Y., Weber, C., Keil, J., and Franke, T., 2009, Real-time rendering of skin changes caused by emotions. In *Intelligent Virtual Agents: 9th International Conference, IVA 2009* (Heidelberg), Springer, pp. 504–505.
43. Kreibig, S. D. (2010). Autonomic nervous system activity in emotion: A review. *Biological Psychology*, 84(3), 394-421.

Regarding someone who is embarrassed, his face first reddens and then whitens.... When he becomes embarrassed it is first... as if he is filled with anger, and his face becomes red. Then, when he is unable to find a way to get rid of this embarrassment from upon his face, he panics inside [*do'eg be-kirbo*]...and his face becomes white.

Rav Bartenura is describing a progression of the emotions a person may experience when confronted with a humiliating situation. At first he may be angry, which, as researchers have noted, serves a certain protective function. If a person is embarrassed and his self-identity is threatened, the expression of anger can lead the aggressor to back off,[44] thus restoring his sense of security. When this anger is ineffective, and the embarrassed party recognizes that he cannot escape from the humiliation, a sense of panic or fear may set in. This panic, as with other types of panic, can trigger the fight or flight response, leading to the effect of a pale-face. If this is correct, we see a remarkable insight emerging from Chazal, which is harmonious with the contemporary understanding of emotion in general, and the specific experience of humiliation in particular. An embarrassing experience may involve a variety of distressing emotional responses, depending on the circumstances of the event, the offender, and the victim. There may be anger, shame, embarrassment, fear or panic, or any combination of these or other emotions, and each of these responses may have external expressions on a person's face and overall physiology.

---

44. E.g., Likierman, M. (1987). The function of anger in human conflict. *International Review of Psycho-Analysis, 14,* 143-161.; Novaco, R. W. (1976). The functions and regulation of the arousal of anger. *American Journal of Psychiatry, 133*(10), 1124-1128.

This recognition of the punishing nature of the physiological aspects of emotions is also expressed in halachic contexts. Of course, causing another person emotional distress that can be discerned externally on his face, be it in the form of shame or fear, is considered a severe violation. However, the following passage demonstrates to what extent the Rabbis were sensitive to the humiliation of others, particularly the type of humiliation that would lead to physiological effects. The Gemara cites the statement of Rabbi Ammi and Rabbi Asi:

> When Rav Dimi came from the land of Israel, he said: From where is it derived that with regard to one who is owed one hundred dinars by another and knows that the borrower does not have the funds to repay him, that it is prohibited for him to pass before the borrower, [so as not to embarrass the borrower and cause him discomfort]? The verse states: "Do not be to him as a creditor" (*Bava Metzia* 75b).

Rabbi Ammi and Rabbi Asi both say that if one upsets another in this way, it is as though he sentences him to two types of punishments, as it is stated: "You have caused men to ride over our heads; we went through fire and through water." The mere presence of the creditor, in an instance that the debtor is unable to pay, is a source of humiliation, and by passing before the debtor, the creditor is considered to be generating these forms of severe punishment for the debtor. With this *halachah*, the Sages are identifying both a deep sensitivity to psychological vulnerability of those in need, as well as the moral implications of such an understanding.

Lesson for Today

During any intake, the first question I ask is, "What brings you in today?" It is not uncommon for someone to point to some type of physical symptom—physical pain, tension in the back or shoulders, periodic elevated heart-rate, or even frequent blushing—as a primary concern that pushed him to seek therapy. While some people connect the distressing physical sensations to a specific emotional or psychological state, many others do not have a clear understanding of the connection between specific emotions and physiological changes. In such cases, a useful part of therapy is psychoeducation about the relationship between emotions and physiological changes, and how being mindful of the physical symptoms can be helpful to their progress in therapy.

Awareness of one's physiological changes can serve a number of useful purposes. For example, early in my training I was part of a team working with a person who, in the course of a manic episode, had demonstrated extremely aggressive and violent behavior towards friends and family members. After a period of time in an inpatient facility, and an adjustment of her medication, she was ready to return home and try to rebuild her relationships. What her treatment team observed, however, is that even the thought of returning home triggered a sense of humiliation and shame, as she anticipated facing the people who saw her in such a difficult state; as a result, she, in one way or another, would sabotage her release from the inpatient facility, which allowed her to delay the inevitable reunion with those she had harmed. Whenever the topic of her return home came up, her cheeks would turn red, she turned her eyes down, and she began to speak in a quiet voice—all indications of her experience of humiliation, even though, at first, she was unable to articulate that this was her emotional state. As is the case with many of us, her instinct was to find a way out of this extremely unpleasant emotional or psychological state—the feeling of humiliation; she found temporary relief through engaging in behaviors that would ensure she could remain in the inpatient facility for a little while longer. Eventually, through work with a psychologist, this patient began to use the physical changes associated with humiliation—blushing, averting gaze, lowering her voice—as cues to her experience, which allowed her to see the connection between her sense of humiliation and the disruptive behaviors she was exhibiting; this awareness opened the door for her to be able to learn more effective coping skills, return home, and effectively face the humiliating experience of owning up to her previous behavior. Just as her awareness of her emotional experience and reactions to those emotions was helpful to her progress, the more we can be aware of our own emotional experience and subsequent reactions the more effectively we can bring to bear healthy coping skills to manage challenging situations or interactions.

In addition to the benefit we may see for ourselves by gaining more awareness of our emotional states, we may also infer from Chazal's focus on physiological changes associated with humiliation another profound benefit of this phenomenon. Imagine for a moment that our emotions had no physical or external manifestations—how would we be able to discern what another person is experiencing? How would we know to instruct the creditor not to pass before his debtor? How would we know when our friend or family member is sad, ashamed, disappointed, upset, or frustrated? How would we know whether they are experiencing joy or excitement? A person who experiences emotional pain or joy exclusively on the inside loses the opportunity to connect to others through these emotions, and others risk causing this person emotional distress without knowing it. By showing one's emotions outwardly, others are able to see when something they say or do is harming another person and then take the steps to rectify their actions. Seeing the effects of our misdeeds can prompt us to become more compassionate, sensitive people to others who are in vulnerable positions, and to treat them with the care and respect that they deserve.

80% of Life is Just Showing Up
Chazal's Secret for Longevity (8a)

אָמְרוּ לֵיהּ לְרַבִּי יוֹחָנָן אִיכָּא סָבֵי בְּבָבֶל תָּמַהּ...
כֵּיוָן דְּאָמְרִי לֵיהּ מְקַדְּמֵי וּמְחַשְּׁכֵי לְבֵי כְנִישְׁתָּא אָמַר הַיְינוּ דְּאַהֲנֵי לְהוּ

The Sages said to Rabbi Yochanan: "there are elders in Babylonia"; he was confounded...When they told him that people in Babylonia going early in the morning and late in the evening to the synagogue, he said "That is what is effective for them to have a long life."

In 2018, a blogger curious about what lifestyle tips contribute to long life decided to mine interviews with centenarians, whose minds remained sufficiently intact, to find out how they explained their own longevity.[45] Some advice was intuitive, like the guidance provided by Mary Todisco, aged 103:

I watch my weight—no sugar, honey. If life's not good today, forget about it. Tomorrow, it will be better. Look at it that way. Let it go by. Keep yourself occupied and busy. Do that all the time.

---

45. Retrieved from https://www.aplaceformom.com/blog/senior-information/how-to-live-to-100/.

Other centenarians highlighted practices that seem surprising, even to doctors. Around 15% of those interviewed recommended consuming alcohol regularly, roughly 30% advocated for disregarding standard dietary recommendations, and several suggested that smoking cigarettes or cigars contributed to their durability. Perhaps these responses should be best understood in light of the comment by David Epstein regarding athletes who display remarkable abilities: "Just because you're a bird doesn't mean you're an ornithologist."[46] In other words, just because someone has lived a long time does not mean that he or she is an expert in how to achieve longevity.

While a day barely goes by without a new piece of advice from scientists or medical professionals aimed at how someone can extend life, it is worth considering how Chazal addressed this fundamental question. Some sources are in line with what we may consider intuitive, such as how Rabbi Yonah Gerondi (Rabbeinu Yonah) interprets the following Mishnah in *Pirkei Avos* (2:7): "The more flesh, the more worms. The more possessions, the more worry.... The more Torah, the more life." Rabbeinu Yonah explains:

> "The more Torah, the more life" is in contrast to the previous statement of "the more flesh, the more worms," as indulging in physical pleasures shorten a person's life, and through toil in Torah a person's life is extended. The statement is also in contrast to the statement "the more possessions, the more worry," because worry about one's property shortens one's life.

46. Epstein, D. (2014). *The sports gene: Inside the science of extraordinary athletic performance.* New York, NY. Penguin.

Rabbeinu Yonah, in interpreting this Mishnah, identifies two factors commonly cited in the effort of living longer, healthier lives: eating right, and reducing psychological stress. However, a Midrash parallel to the Gemara in *Berachos* (8a) identifies a surprising practice that they suggest contributes to longevity:

> Rebbi told Rabbi Yochanan that there are elders in Babylonia, he was confounded and said: It is written: "So that your days will be lengthened and the days of your children upon the land the Lord swore to your forefathers to give to them like the days of heaven on the earth" (*Devarim* 11:21); lengthened in the land of Israel but not outside of the Land. Why then, do the residents of Babylonia live long lives? When they told him that the people in Babylonia go early in the morning and go late in the evening to the synagogue, he said: That is what was effective for them in extending their lives.
>
> As Rabbi Yehoshua ben Levi said to his sons: Go up early and leave early so that your lives will be extended and your learning will remain intact (*Yalkut Shimoni, Eikev* 871).

The Gemara sources this guarantee from *Mishlei* (8:34-35) "Happy is the man who listens to Me, watching daily at My gates, guarding at My door posts... for whoso finds Me finds life and obtains the favor of the Lord." Although the verse refers to life, and the Gemara seems to interpret this statement in its physical sense, the Midrash expands the blessing to retaining one's knowledge of Torah, the source of spiritual life. In today's language, these blessings—which are conferred by attending synagogue morning and evening—might be referred to as longevity and neurocognitive integrity.

How or why does daily synagogue attendance contribute to such blessing? It is possible that the mechanism ensuring the verse's promise of a long life is strictly a spiritual or metaphysical one, namely that someone who demonstrates the commitment to attend synagogue regularly merits a reward of extended life and an intact mind. Being part of a *tzibbur* (community), particularly in the context of prayer, grants a certain protection to the community members, as codified by Rambam:

> Communal prayer is always heard. Even when there are transgressors among [the congregation], the Holy One, blessed be He, does not reject the prayers of the many. Therefore, a person should include himself in the community and should not pray alone whenever he is able to pray with the community. One should always spend the early morning and evening [hours] in the synagogue, for prayer [is always heard when recited] in the synagogue. Anyone who has a synagogue in his city and does not enter it to pray is called a bad neighbor (*Hilchos Tefillah* 8:1; see also *Hilchos Teshuvah* 2:6).[47]

---

47. Later commentators debate the relationship between praying with a *minyan* and praying in a synagogue. For example, see *Tzlach, Berachos* 6a, and *Mishnah Berurah* 90:28. Nevertheless, it is clear from Rambam, based on the Gemara (*Berachos* 6a), that one's prayers are more effective when offered with a *tzibbur*, even if that *tzibbur* is known to be imperfect.

Chazal also taught that being part of a *tzibbur* confers other benefits, as highlight by the following Gemara:

> Rav Shmuel bar Inya said in the name of Rav: From where is it derived that [regarding] the sentence of a community... although it is sealed, it can still be torn up? As it is stated: "As is the Lord our God whenever we call out to Him" ... [which is referring to] a community (*Rosh Hashanah* 18a).

In other words, Rav Shmuel bar Inya is teaching that there are times that a community's negative fate is sealed, but through the communal prayer and *teshuvah* (repentance), that decree can be overturned. Of course, the implication of this lesson is that beneficiaries of this reversal are those who are part of this *tzibbur*.

In addition to these metaphysical benefits of participating in communal prayer and activity, it is also possible that there are physical mechanisms through which the promise of long life and sustained wisdom is realized. Contemporary medical and psychological research may provide valuable insight into different ways through which, for the elderly, regular synagogue attendance may be beneficial.

Aerobic Exercise

Dr. Kenneth Cooper, often referred to as "the father of aerobics," famously wrote that "you do not stop exercising because you get old; you get old because you stop exercising." Since his book *Aerobics* came out in 1968, researchers have studied the direct effects of aerobic exercise on aging, with two primary areas of focus: longevity and neurocognitive functioning. To obtain these benefits, the USA government recommends 2.5-5 hours per week (or 20-40 minutes per day) of moderate intensity exercise for adults 65 years and older,[48] which can include brisk walking. Studies have consistently shown that people who engage in physical activity see substantial benefits to a variety of physiological systems, including cardiovascular health, and reduction in systemic inflammation. Various studies have shown that physical activity among older adults can play a role in the prevention, management, or treatment of a variety of conditions, including arthritis, cancer, coronary artery disease, depression, physical disability, hypertension, obesity, osteoporosis, peripheral vascular disease, stroke, and type 2 diabetes.[49] Additional studies consistently have demonstrated exercise's benefit regarding neurocognitive functioning.[50] For example, even among younger adults, aerobic exercise is associated with improved attention and processing speed, executive function, and memory.[51] Notably,

---

48. Retrieved from https://health.gov/paguidelines/second-edition/pdf/Physical_Activity_Guidelines_2nd_edition.pdf.
49. Chodzko-Zajko, W. J., Proctor, D. N., Singh, M. A. F., Minson, C. T., Nigg, C. R., Salem, G. J., & Skinner, J. S. (2009). Exercise and physical activity for older adults. *Medicine & Science in Sports & Exercise, 41*(7), 1510-1530.
50. Hillman, C. H., Erickson, K. I., & Kramer, A. F. (2008). Be smart, exercise your heart: Exercise effects on brain and cognition. *Nature Reviews Neuroscience, 9*(1), 58.
51. Smith, P. J., Blumenthal, J. A., Hoffman, B. M., Cooper, H., Strauman, T. A., Welsh-Bohmer, K., ... & Sherwood, A. (2010). Aerobic exercise and neurocognitive performance: A meta-analytic review of randomized controlled trials. *Psychosomatic Medicine, 72*(3), 239.

according to recent estimates, only around 10% of adults in USA over the age of 70 meet the daily exercise requirements.[52]

As this very brief survey of a few recent studies highlights, aerobic exercise has a profound positive impact on many aspects of physical, psychological, and cognitive functioning. An important question is whether synagogue attendance for older adults would constitute aerobic exercise. In the times of the Gemara, synagogues were often located in the fields, outside of the residential neighborhoods (see, e.g., *Tur* 236:2). While for a younger person walking to the synagogue for services may not be considered aerobic exercise, this type of walking would probably constitute aerobic exercise for older people. Indeed, it seems likely that twice-daily synagogue attendance would include at least 20 minutes of walking each day, and would go a long way toward meeting the recommendations for adequate physical activity for older adults. Admittedly, this explanation may seem somewhat far-fetched that the physical activity of walking to *shul* would contribute to such an increase in longevity; nevertheless, at the very least, such activity would deter older adults from maintaining a sedentary lifestyle that may be likely for people who are no longer active members of the workforce.

Loneliness

In 2018, Theresa May, the Prime Minister of the United Kingdom, appointed a "minister for loneliness." This minister would be

---

52. Tucker, J. M., Welk, G. J., & Beyler, N. K. (2011). Physical activity in US adults: Compliance with the physical activity guidelines for Americans. *American Journal of Preventive Medicine*, 40(4), 454-461.

charged to provide support for the millions of Britons who endorsed feeling lonely, including up to 200,000 older adults who had not had a conversation with a friend or family member in over a month.[53] This concern was echoed by a previous USA Surgeon General, Vivek Murthy:[54]

> During my years caring for patients, the most common pathology I saw was not heart disease or diabetes; it was loneliness. Loneliness and weak social connections are associated with a reduction in lifespan similar to that caused by smoking 15 cigarettes a day and even greater than that associated with obesity. Loneliness is also associated with a greater risk of cardiovascular disease, dementia, depression, and anxiety.

In psychological literature, the sense of belonging is considered a fundamental drive and need for people of all ages.[55] The centrality of social engagement may be particularly salient for older adults as, in one study, older adults more often named social engagement than mentioned physical health as a feature of successful aging,[56]

53. Retrieved from https://www.gov.uk/government/news/pm-launches-governments-first-loneliness-strategy.
54 Murthy, V. (2017). Work and the loneliness epidemic. *Harvard Business Review, 9.*
55. Baumeister, R. F., & Leary, M. R. (1995). The need to belong: Desire for interpersonal attachments as a fundamental human motivation. *Psychological Bulletin, 117*(3), 497.
56. Depp, C. A., & Jeste, D. V. (2006). Definitions and predictors of successful aging: A comprehensive review of larger quantitative studies. *The American Journal of Geriatric Psychiatry, 14*(1), 6-20.

and experts are increasingly recognizing the tremendous burden loneliness places on the medical, economic, and social systems.[57] Indeed, part of Theresa May's plan for the UK is to encourage general practitioners to engage in a practice knowns as "social prescribing," which means to refer older adults suffering from loneliness to "a variety of activities, such as cookery classes, walking clubs and art groups," instead of services within the medical system.

Feeling a part of a social community for people at any age may be both challenging and important, but for older adults, a number of factors may make developing a sense of community more difficult. For example, family members and close friends may have passed away; others may have moved to another city to be closer to their children; some may develop health or physical mobility limitations which prohibit them from being able to maintain meaningful relationships with friends or family members. As a result, it is understandable that a common challenge faced by older adults is a sense of loneliness and disconnection from other people. In one large longitudinal study (i.e., research that follows people over time, rather than only studying them at a single point in time), researchers found that up to a third of previously not-lonely people develop significant levels of loneliness between ages 60-86. This change is associated with a number of life changes, such as losing a partner, a decline in social activity, and an increase in physical disabilities, among other identified challenges.[58] As mobility becomes limited

---

57. Cacioppo, J. T., & Cacioppo, S. (2018). The growing problem of loneliness. *The Lancet, 391*(10119), 426.

58 Aartsen, M., & Jylhä, M. (2011). Onset of loneliness in older adults: results of a 28 year prospective study. *European Journal of Ageing,* 8(1), 31-38.

and they are not able to work in the same way as they once were,[59] many older adults, particularly older older-adults may spend more time alone with limited social relationships.[60] Recent studies have found that loneliness is associated with higher mortality rates, and may be both a cause and effect of declines in emotional, physical, and functional health.[61]

In short, contemporary science has found that, at least in the Western world, older adults are at substantial risk to experience high levels of loneliness, and this reality presents a significant risk to their physical, mental, and emotional health. Similar to Theresa May's proposal for social prescribing, synagogue attendance for older adults may help to combat loneliness. The synagogue, known as a *beis kenesses*, which literally means "house of gathering," can provide an opportunity for people, especially older people, to maintain social connectedness. As is common in synagogues around the world, worshippers often engage in friendly chatter before and after services (and perhaps even during services), and friendships can be formed or sustained during these interactions. People may invite others over to their homes for Shabbos or Yom Tov meals, or coordinate other social activities with each other. Additionally, if someone is

---

59. Buchman, A. S., Boyle, P. A., Wilson, R. S., James, B. D., Leurgans, S. E., Arnold, S. E., & Bennett, D. A. (2010). Loneliness and the rate of motor decline in old age: The rush memory and aging project, a community-based cohort study. *BMC Geriatrics*, 10(1), 77.

60. Pinquart, M., & Sorensen, S. (2001). Influences on loneliness in older adults: A meta-analysis. *Basic and Applied Social Psychology*, 23(4), 245-266.

61. Luo, Y., Hawkley, L. C., Waite, L. J., & Cacioppo, J. T. (2012). Loneliness, health, and mortality in old age: A National Longitudinal Study. *Social Science & Medicine* (1982), 74(6), 907.

absent due to an illness or personal issue, other congregants take note and can check up on the missing person. Given all of these factors that seem likely to reduce the likelihood of loneliness, regular *shul* attendance may be a mechanism to combat loneliness and contribute to greater longevity and cognitive integrity.

Sense of Meaning or Purpose

Jewish thought has long emphasized the importance of continuing to be productive into older age. On the verse, "In the morning sow your seed and in the evening do not be idle..." (*Koheles* 11:6), Rashi comments:

> If you studied Torah in your youth, study Torah when you are older; if you had students in your youth, have students when you are older; if you married a woman of child-bearing age in your youth, marry a woman of child-bearing age when you are older; if you were charitable in your youth, be charitable when you are older.

This verse provides an aspirational view of how we might conduct ourselves as we age—instead of only reflecting on our accomplishments of our youth, we are instructed to try our best to continue to be spiritually productive into our later years.

Although the verse indicates that one reason is that we cannot be sure which of our actions—those in youth or those in older age—will have a greater impact, contemporary research suggests that there may be psychological, emotional, and physical benefit to maintaining a productive and meaningful lifestyle as we age, known as "eudaimonic wellbeing."[62] For older adults who are no longer responsible for raising children, and who may not be part of the workforce, finding a sense of purpose in life can be crucial to their physical and mental health as they age.[63] Indeed, a large longitudinal study found that among older adults, those with lowest sense of eudaimonic wellbeing had a mortality rate roughly three times as high as those with the highest levels of eudaimonic wellbeing over an 8.5 year period.[64]

Regular synagogue attendance can add a tremendous amount of purpose to the lives of older adults. They can feel connected to spiritual life as they contribute to the religious activity in their local community, in addition to the social aspect mentioned above. Older men can experience meaning through contributing to the required *minyan* (prayer quorum), which in many places, particularly smaller communities, relies on retired people to be the consistent participants ensuring the presence of a quorum of worshippers and performing ritual duties during the services, such as being the *chazzan* (prayer leader) or *baal koreh* (person who reads the Torah in *shul*). Older men and women can contribute significantly to the synagogue's spiritual life, through creating a stronger community for prayer, mentoring younger community members, serving on *shul*

---

62. Ryan, R. M., & Deci, E. L. (2001). On happiness and human potentials: A review of research on hedonic and eudaimonic wellbeing. *Annual Review of Psychology*, 52(1), 141-166.

63. Irving, J., Davis, S., & Collier, A. (2017). Aging with purpose: Systematic search and review of literature pertaining to older adults and purpose. *The International Journal of Aging and Human Development*, 85(4), 403-437.

64. Steptoe, A., Deaton, A., & Stone, A. A. (2015). Subjective wellbeing, health, and ageing. *The Lancet*, 385(9968), 640-648.

boards or committees, offering classes, helping to set up *kiddush* (meal after services on Shabbos), and any number of other important and necessary roles that benefit the shul and larger community.

Lesson for Today

Neither Rabbi Yochanan nor Rabbi Yehoshua ben Levi offer an explanation regarding why daily synagogue attendance contributes to the congregants' physical and cognitive health, although Chazal were clear that being a part of a community can bestow great spiritual benefits and protections. In addition to the metaphysical advantages, three features that have been discussed in contemporary medical and psychology research may help shed light on possible physical explanations for such a connection, namely physical exercise, decrease in loneliness, and an increased sense of purpose and meaning. What scientists have identified in the past 20-plus years, and what the British government is hoping to institute as part of their healthcare system, is reflected in the practice of the Jewish community for thousands of years; being regularly involved in social and meaningful physical activities can be extremely beneficial for the well-being of aging adults.

I still recall the perennial awkwardness I felt reciting the part of the *Selichos* service during which we echo King David and pray for Hashem to support us as we age: "Do not cast me off in time of old age; when my strength fails, forsake me not" (*Tehillim* 71:9). Of course, all sorts of ailments, injuries, or negative events could befall me in the coming year, but certainly none of them would be a result of old age! The universal practice (at least among Ashkenazi congregations) to recite this prayer out loud in response to the Chazzan, with the

Aron Kodesh (Torah's ark) open, also placed a strange emphasis on it—I often had difficulty feeling the urgency that comes with prayers offered in such a way, because it seemed so distant and not relevant to the prayers I was offering that time of year.

As the years have passed, I have reflected on this prayer and how I relate to it, and two approaches related to this chapter have helped me connect better to this prayer in the *Selichos* service. On an individual level, praying for Hashem's continued support as we age requires us to do our part in achieving that end; after all, based on several passages in the Gemara (e.g., *Berachos* 60a, *Shabbos* 32a), the accepted practice is that we do not pray for miracles. As such, offering this prayer as we are focused on repentance each year requires us to consider what changes we can make to our lives to ensure, with Hashem's help, that we can have as productive and meaningful older age as possible. On a communal level, this prayer may have more immediate implications. If we pray to Hashem to support to us all as we age, we may also ask ourselves what we are doing to help older adults in our own communities, and to help set ourselves up for successful older age. The self-reflective questions generated by this prayer compel us to consider different ways of engaging with others in our communities. Am I keeping myself physically healthy, and can I help older adults in my community increase physical activity? Are there ways for me to increase my engagement with my community and build positive social relationships, and are there ways we can make our communal life more friendly to older adults? Do I possess or am I sharpening skills that will allow me to be and feel productive in my older age, and how can we help provide spaces for older adults to contribute in meaningful ways to the social or spiritual life of our communities?

Due to the pressures of daily life, it is often easy to forget about older adults in our communities who may be find themselves with diminished access to opportunities for social connection and communal involvement. Each one of us, at any age, can play a role in improving our synagogue's and community's openness to people of all ages, which will make our communities that much stronger, and improve the lives of the older adults in our congregations. If synagogues come together to support the participation of older members of the communities in prayer and other communal activities, we can also hope to see the fulfillment of the Torah's promise for a long and meaningful life.

Do You See What I See?

Cultural Differences and the Color of *Techeiles* (9b)

דַּבֵּר אֶל בְּנֵי יִשְׂרָאֵל וְאָמַרְתָּ אֲלֵהֶם וְעָשׂוּ לָהֶם
צִיצִת עַל כַּנְפֵי בִגְדֵיהֶם לְדֹרֹתָם וְנָתְנוּ עַל צִיצִת הַכָּנָף פְּתִיל תְּכֵלֶת

"Speak to the Children of Israel and say to them that they shall make themselves tzitzis on the corners of their garments, throughout their generations. And they shall place upon the tzitzis of each corner a thread of techeiles." — Bamidbar 15:38

One of the most memorable viral trends in recent years started in a very unexpected way. A bride-to-be posted a photograph on Facebook of the dress her mother was going to wear, and a debate ensued between friends regarding the dress's color: was it white and gold, or blue and black? Following the wedding, on February 26, 2015, a friend of the bride posted the picture to her social media page, and from there it went viral. After just one week, more than 10 million comments on social media had referenced the dress, and the original news article covering the breaking story had over 37 million reads. There was international interest, as many celebrities weighed in with their perception, and fierce debate raged on social media sites with people adamantly defending their positions.

Neuroscientists and psychologists were summoned to try to explain how it is possible that people, looking at the same photo, could see two dramatically different color schemes. Articles appeared in academic or professional journals providing theories and data regarding this unusual phenomenon.[65] Somehow, it is possible for two people to observe the same photograph and identify two completely different sets of colors.

As described in other chapters in this volume, any student of Talmud and *halachah* quickly realizes the relevance of many aspects of psychology on the application of *halachah* to real-life situations. However, less frequently are there principles that emerge from psychology that can explain various statements or halachic rulings of Chazal. Indeed, as it relates to the color of *techeiles*, findings

---

65. For examples from several journals see Winkler, A. D., Spillmann, L., Werner, J. S., & Webster, M. A. (2015). Asymmetries in blue–yellow color perception and in the color of 'the dress'. *Current Biology*, 25(13), R547-R548; Rabin, J., Houser, B., Talbert, C., & Patel, R. (2016). Blue-black or white-gold? Early stage processing and the color of 'the dress'. *PloS One*, 11(8), e0161090; Chetverikov, A., & Ivanchei, I. (2016). Seeing "the Dress" in the right light: Perceived colors and inferred light sources. *Perception*, 45(8), 910-930; Wallisch, P. (2017). Illumination assumptions account for individual differences in the perceptual interpretation of a profoundly ambiguous stimulus in the color domain: "The dress". *Journal of Vision*, 17(4), 5-5; Vemuri, K., Bisla, K., Mulpuru, S., & Varadharajan, S. (2016). Do normal pupil diameter differences in the population underlie the color selection of the dress?. *Journal of the Optical Society of America A*, 33(27), A137; Melgosa, M., Gómez-Robledo, L., Isabel Suero, M., & Fairchild, M. D. (2015). What can we learn from a dress with ambiguous colors?. *Color Research & Application*, 40(5), 525-529.

by psychological researchers in the past 50 years can shed light on comments in the Talmud and Rishonim that were previously difficult to understand.

To some extent, color is not an issue of psychology or perception, but a matter of physics and wavelengths. On average, the human eye can perceive light at wavelengths between roughly 390-700 nanometers, which is the color spectrum ranging from violet to red. However, over the past 50 years, cross-cultural researchers have noted that the way that people perceive color, and the language they use to describe it, differs drastically across various cultures and populations. Many colors that we typically regard as distinct are in various cultures either described by identical terms, or, in some cases, perceived to be the same hue. For example, a great deal of recent research has focused on comparing Westerners with members of the Himba tribe of Namibia; whereas researchers have identified 11 distinct color categories among American English speakers, the Himba tribe has only 5. Similarly, sometimes significant disagreement can arise about how to characterize items of a specific hue. As we will describe below, differences in color perception and description may play a role in discrepancies regarding *techeiles,* both in the Gemara, as well as by later Rishonim.

Color of Techeiles in Rambam

Interest in the color of *techeiles* among the larger Jewish community has increased in recent decades as many believe that the long-lost *chilazon* (a certain type of snail) that produced the dye has been found. *Techeiles* is used for the strands of *tzitzis,* as the verse commands: "They shall make themselves *tzitzis* on the corners of their garments, throughout their generations. And they shall place upon the *tzitzis* of each corner a thread of *techeiles*" (*Bamidbar* 15:38). Most translations understand that the color described in the Torah should be translated as "blue," and, according to the ArtScroll translation, this color refers to "turquoise." However, despite these ubiquitous definitions, it is not entirely clear that these definitions are how the Rishonim described this color.

In truth, the uncertainty regarding how to describe the color begins in the Talmud. Famously, the Gemara records Rabbi Meir's explanation for the purpose of *techeiles* on our fringes:

> Because *techeiles* resembles the color of the sea, and the sea resembles the color of the sky, and the sky resembles the color of [a sapphire, and a sapphire resembles the color of] the Throne of Glory, as it is said, "And there was under his feet as it were a paved work of sapphire stone" (*Shemos* 24:10), and it is also written, "The likeness of a throne as the appearance of a sapphire stone" (*Yechezkel* 1:26; *Menachos* 43b).

However, the Talmud Yerushalmi (*Berachos* 1:2) cites a slightly different version of Rabbi Meir's statement. In that version, the *techeiles* is similar to the sea, which is similar to *assavim* (some type of vegetation), and the *assavim* are similar to the sky, and the sky is similar to the Throne of Glory, which is similar to a sapphire. Presumably, there was not a disagreement about the actual hue of the *techeiles*. After all, both statements agree that *techeiles* can be compared to the sky and sapphire; the discrepant versions appear to differ on what colors or items are best representative of *techeiles*, or at least what can be considered in the same color family.

Additional disagreements about the color of *techeiles* continued through the times of the Rishonim. According to Rambam, the color of *techeiles* seems to be sky-blue, as he describes its color as some type of *kachol,* and continues that it is "the color of the sky which appears opposite the sun when there is a clear sky" (*Hilchos Tzitzis* 2:1). However, a later *halachah* appears to provide a different understanding:

> When a garment is entirely red, green, or any other color [besides white], its "white" strands should be made from the same color as the garment itself. If it is *yarok* (usually translated as "green"), they should be *yarok.* If it is red, they should be red. Should the garment itself be *techeiles,* its white strands should be made from **any color other than black for it resembles *techeiles*** (*Hilchos Tzitzis* 2:8).

As the *Kesef Mishneh* notes, this is not a direct quote from the Gemara in *Menachos* (41b), which states that if an entire garment is made with *techeiles,* then the "white" strands may not be colored with *kalah ilan,* which is a dye that the Gemara considers identical in color to *techeiles.* The *Kesef Mishneh,* in his second view explaining why Rambam specifies that the non-*techeiles* strings cannot be black, suggests that Rambam's position is because black is similar enough to *techeiles* that there would be insufficient contrast between the *techeiles* and the other strings. For the average westerner, this argument seems strange—is black really similar enough to *techeiles,* such that the two would be as indistinguishable as *techeiles* with *kalah ilan*? What about dark shades of other colors, like green or purple—are those less similar to *techeiles* than black?

Color of Techeiles in Rashi

In contrast to Rambam's description, Rashi appears to offer a different description of *techeiles*, which Rashi defines in two different ways in the same passage. In one place, Rashi (on *Bamidbar* 15:38) explains that the color is *yarok*, which is typically understood to be green.[66] It is possible that Rashi's commentary is based on his understanding of the Mishnah (*Berachos* 9b) which states that according to one opinion, the earliest time to recite *keriyas Shema* is when there is enough light to discern between *techeiles* and white, or, according to Rabbi Eliezer, between *techeiles* and *karti*. *Karti* is understood to be referring to a leek, which is green, and Rashi comments that *techeiles* "is green, and it is close to *karti*." Rashi seems to learn that *techeiles* is something similar to green, such that one would need more significant light to discern between the two.

However, several verses later Rashi himself writes that the *techeiles* is reminiscent of the destruction of the Egyptians which happened at night, and the color is like the color of "sky that blackens in the evening." For Rashi's internal logic, this explanation is puzzling: how can something be both green, and similar to the darkening night sky? Additionally, on its face, this interpretation seems to be in opposition of Rambam's description that *techeiles* is similar the daytime sky; counterintuitively, Rambam, who describes *techeiles* as the color of a bright blue sky compares it to black, while Rashi who compares it to the evening or night sky does not draw that comparison.

---

66. The term *yarok* also can mean yellow, and a full discussion of this issue requires its own chapter. As a starting point, see, for example, Tosafos, *Sukkah* 31b, and the sources he cites, as well as the sources discussed here regarding the topic of the discolored lung.

Kachol vs. Shachor

In addition to the question of the color of *techeiles*, a related issue also may be an area of controversy, namely the relationship between *kachol* and *shachor*. The Gemara depicts the beauty of the renovations to the *Beis Ha-Mikdash* (Holy Temple) by Herod:

> It used to be said: He who has not seen the Temple of Herod has never seen a beautiful building. Of what did he build it? Rabbah said: stones of *shisha* and *marmerah*. Some say, of **kuchlah,** *shishah* and *marmerah*. Alternate rows [of the stones] projected, so as to leave a place for cement. He originally intended to cover it with gold, but the Rabbis advised him not to, since it was more beautiful as it was, looking like the waves of the sea (*Bava Basra* 4a).

At first glance, the Rabbis in the Gemara thought that the building's façade made of alternative stones was beautiful, and thus requested that the walls not be covered by gold; however, Maharsha and others point to a deeper meaning. He explained that the Rabbis, presumably because of the *kuchlah*, were referring to Rabbi Meir's chain of associations listed above, and that being reminded of Hashem's glory and majesty was appropriate for anyone entering the Holy Temple.

According to Rashi, the word *kuchlah*[67] refers to a stone the color

67. According to various sources, including Jastrow's dictionary, *kochal* refers to stibium (or stibnite), which is also called antimony. This mineral was used in ancient times in powder form as black eye-makeup. Mineral and gem experts say that the color of stibnite can range from "tin-white with a blueish tinge," lead gray, bluish lead

of *kachol,* which we would typically translate as "blue."[68] In contrast, Rabbi Gershom ben Yehudah (Rabbeinu Gershom) defined *kuchlah* as *shechorin,* "black." It is possible that Rabbeinu Gershom, who lived around the year 1000 C.E., does not subscribe to Maharsha's explanation, and therefore he defined the color of *kuchlah* in accordance with its usage as a cosmetic. However, if we assume that Rabbeinu Gershom agrees with Maharsha's interpretation, this would point to another example from the Rishonim of comparing black with the blue color of the sky and sapphires.

A similar *machlokes* between Rambam and Rashi about how to categorize the color blue—as either a type of black or not—can be found in their commentaries on a separate topic in the Talmud. The Gemara describes what types of abnormalities in the lungs of an animal render it a *treifah* (an animal unfit for consumption due to an illness) (*Chullin* 47b). The Gemara records the following statement:

Rava said: If [the lung was] *kuchlah* it is permitted, if black like ink it is *treifah*; for Rabbi Chanina said: Black [blood] is [in reality] red blood which has turned black by disease.

---

gray, steel gray, and black. Apparently, before it oxidizes, there is a noticeable blue color, but after it oxidizes the color changes to black. *Aruch Ha-Shulchan* (*Yoreh De'ah* 38:8) seems to have been aware of this characteristic. He states that Rashi's explanation is pre-oxidized (or "before placing the stone in water") whereas Rambam is referring to *kuchlah* in its post-oxidized state.

68. Although blue is not how Rashi define *techeiles,* it seems likely that he would agree that a blue color would also be reminiscent of the chain of associations mentioned in *Menachos.*

According to Rashi, *kuchlah* refers to "the color of *kachol*, which is like *lazur* in our language [i.e., Old French],[69] which is neither *yarok* nor black." Rambam, however, adds an additional qualifier not found in the text of the Gemara:

> There are five forbidden hues for the lung: black like ink…
> There are four permitted hues [for the lung]. They are:
> Black like *kochal*…(*Hilchos Shechitah* 7:17, 19).

Apparently, Rambam understood Rava's statement to be contrasting two types of colors that can be categorized as black, but it is not clear what drove Rambam to explain the Gemara in such a way. It is possible that Rambam is basing his comment on a textual source; if so, this source could be a Midrash (*Bamidbar Rabbah* 2:7) describing the stones of each tribe that were found on the *choshen mishpat*, the Kohen Gadol's breastplate (*Shemos* 28:18), which states that Yissachar's stone, the sapphire, is "*shachor* like *kachol*." It is also possible that Rambam assumed that all usages of the term *kachol* refers to oxidized stibium, which is close to black. Additionally, he may have learned it from a *diyuk* (deduction) in Rava's statement, namely that both must be referring to some type of black color, because why else specify "black like ink" and not simply say "black"? Whatever the reason, Rambam added this interpretation into the Gemara even though other Rishonim were not compelled to understand it in the same way.

---

69. This word is probably similar to English word "azure," a type of blue. According to Merriam-Webster, the word "azure" can be traced back through Middle-English, French English, and Old Spanish, and ultimately to the Arabic and Persian words "lazaward."

Cross-cultural Features of Color Perception

What emerges according to these sources is several difficulties both in reconciling various Talmudic passages, as well as the internal logic of the Rishonim, with the questions that are left to be resolved:

1. According to Rambam, the color of *techeiles* is referring to the daytime sky on a clear day, and is also a color that can be described as both a type of blue and a shade of black.
2. According to Rashi, *techeiles* is referring to the evening or night sky, but is also a color that can be described as green-ish.
3. The Talmudic tradition of the visual allusions generated by *techeiles* include green in one text but not the other, even though they both seem to agree on the color of *techeiles*.

Using traditional tools of Talmudic analysis, these discrepancies are very difficult to reconcile. However, if we consider findings from modern-day cross-cultural research, we may be able to reach a tentative hypothesis that can shed light on the usage of certain descriptions by the Rabbis of the Talmud, as well as Rambam and Rashi. As previously noted, how we describe colors to others who cannot see them, in the absence of data regarding their wavelengths, requires several elements. We must have the tools to physically perceive that color, our brains must interpret what we are seeing, and we have to decide what color-related words or other commonly known items would best serve as a reference. Each one of these elements can be affected by many differences, including biological, environmental, and cultural. Most relevant for this discussion is the cultural influence of how colors are described to another person.

The human eye and brain can perceive and distinguish between many thousands (if not millions) of colors, but we typically group many colors into color families that share a common descriptor; for example, most people would describe plum, violet, mauve, and aubergine as "purple." The tendency for cultures to group objectively different hues together as one basic color is termed by researchers as exhibiting "semantic color identities," a phenomenon that scientists regard as the rule, and not the exception.[70] In other words, every culture has typical patterns regarding how they group together varying hues; the question is which hues each culture includes in their color groupings.

Some of the most common types of semantic color identities found in cross cultural research is the non-differentiation between blue-black, as well as non-differentiation between green-blue, or green-blue-black.[71] According to this study of 145 separate societies, 50% of the societies had a single word to denote both green and blue, 15% had a single word for both black and blue, and 12% had a single word to denote green, blue, and black.[72] If we apply these findings to the questions above, we can reconcile some of the difficulties.

70. Bornstein, Marc H. "The influence of visual perception on culture." *American Anthropologist* 77.4 (1975): 774-798.
71. For a more contemporary discussion, see Pitchford, Nicola, and Carole P. Biggam, eds. *Progress in Colour Studies: Volume II. Psychological aspects.* John Benjamins Publishing, 2006.
72. For a comprehensive review of many aspects of culture and color perception, see also MacLaury, R. E., Paramei, G. V., & Dedrick, D. (Eds.). (2007). *Anthropology of Color: Interdisciplinary Multilevel Modeling.* John Benjamins Publishing. Although there is no conclusive explanation for these findings, one suggestion with some supporting evidence ties regional exposure to damaging UV rays to patterns of color perception. For example, see Lindsey, D. T., & Brown, A. M. (2002). Color naming and the phototoxic effects of sunlight on the eye. *Psychological Science,* 13(6), 506-512.

Regarding the two versions of Rabbi Meir's chain of recollection, there is no disagreement about the color itself, but there might be a difference of whether green is categorized as a type of blue or as its own distinct color. In the Talmud Bavli's report of Rabbi Meir's statement, perhaps the reporter saw the green of vegetation as a distinct color from the blue of the sea; as such, the color of *techeiles* would not remind someone of the *assavim*. However, in the Talmud Yerushalmi, perhaps the reporter saw green and blue hues as being part of the same color family, so the blue-ish hue of *techeiles* would remind a person of greenery, which would in turn be reminiscent of the sky and sapphires. This view is supported by Rabbi Yaakov ben Moshe Levi Moelin (Maharil), quoted in *Shach* (*Yoreh De'ah* 38), in regard to the discolored lung who says that "*Yarok*—that is called in Ashkenaz either *green* or *blue* is kosher;"[73] in other words, the colors green and blue are described by the Hebrew word *yarok*. According to this approach, it is not green that is part of the blue family, but rather it is blue that is part of the green family.

Rashi apparently thought that some blue hues are their own color group—*kachol*—but that group comprises only the lighter, bright blues. Darker shades of blue, of which *techeiles* is one, are part of the green family, so much so that he did not use the term *kachol* at all to describe *techeiles*, despite the Gemara's comparison of *techeiles* with sapphires. Perhaps for this reason Rashi was compelled to say that *techeiles* is like the night sky, because only the darker shades of blue can be grouped with green, as is done by the Talmud Yerushalmi.

A support for this view of Rashi may come from a comment he makes regarding the color of a flame. The Gemara (*Berachos* 52b)

---

73. The words "green" and "blue" are transliterated in the original text of Maharil

records a disagreement between Beis Hillel and Beis Shammai regarding the proper wording for the blessing over the flame during *Havdalah*. Beis Shammai says the correct word is *"ma'or,"* in singular form, referring to a single light, while Beis Hillel argues that the correct word is *"me'orei,"* in plural, as "there are many lights in the fire." In explaining the position of Beis Hillel, Rashi comments that "the flame has red, white, and *yerakrekes* [from the same word as *yarok*, meaning 'green']." Of course, different types of fuel can produce different color flames; nevertheless, observing the way most of our common fuels burn nowadays (such as olive oil, or wax), the area closest to the wick burns a dark bluish hue, which seems to be what Rashi is referring to with the term *"yerakrekes."*[74] Elsewhere, Rashi uses this term to refer to the green color of sprouting beets (*Eruvin* 53b). It seems that Rashi typically uses this term to describe a green-ish color, which would include what we would call the dark blue part of a flame.

Rambam, however, appears to categorize blue as a type of black, another one of the semantic color identities noted by Bornstein. However, in contrast to Rashi, who distinguishes between light and dark blue, Rambam's designation of black as similar to blue is independent of the lightness or darkness of the blue color. As such, Rambam says that the color of *techeiles* is similar to the color of the daytime sky on a clear day, as well as similar to black. If this is correct,

---

74. It is important to note that Ritva and *Shitah Mekubetzes* have an alternate text of Rashi that includes the color black in the list of colors of the flame. According to their text, *yerakrekes* could be referring to dark blue color seen near the wick, or, alternatively, to the yellow-ish hue seen in the flame; in such a case, this Rashi would not provide support one way or another.

it helps clarify the questions posed above related to the explanation of the *Kesef Mishnah*. Although it may seem unusual from a westerner's perspective who clearly distinguishes between blue and black, for Rambam these two colors are part of the same perceptual family, and, as such, would be regarded as too similar. Regarding other similar colors, such as dark green or dark purple, even though we, in our culture, may perceive them as more similar to *techeiles*, because they are considered separate color families, Rambam would argue that they would be more readily distinguishable from *techeiles* if they were paired together on the corner of a garment.

Lessons for Today

Even though studies in perception remain popular in experimental psychology, it is more difficult to generate life-lessons that emerge directly from these specific studies. Nevertheless, there are two messages, one halachic, and one related to personal development, that can be learned from this line of study. In contemporary Jewish life, color perception plays a central role in at least one prominent aspect of daily life—namely, the laws of *niddah* (family purity). When studying for Rabbinic ordination, many students work with an expert to learn how to examine *mar'os*, or cloths used by women to examine whether there remains any menstrual blood, which would render the woman *temei'ah* (ritually impure). As much as any other area of *halachah*, it is crucial to receive practical instruction from an expert and not rely simply on book learning. In this case, the same word can refer to different visual perceptions, depending on the region, language, or era that the authority is writing in. And these word choices, descriptions, and comparisons can have a profound impact on ruling whether a woman is *tahorah* (ritually pure) or *temei'ah*.

The second lesson, which relates to personal character development, is that of humility. There are probably few things that we would regard more objectively than what color we are looking at, which may explain how the debate over "the dress" escalated so fiercely. Each person was certain that her or his way of seeing was the only way it could possibly be seen. Indeed, when we explain that two things are so obviously different that no further explanation is required, we use colors: "it's a black-and-white issue." And yet, despite this confidence, we see that even in how we perceive colors there is a not a definitive correct way of perceiving these colors. Taking this lesson to heart can help us build patience and empathy for those who see other, less obvious things differently.

So after all this, what color is *techeiles*? It is possible that in reality, both Rambam and Rashi are correct, there is no real argument, and that Rashi and Rambam, upon seeing the same strand of authentic *techeiles*, would produce divergent descriptions.

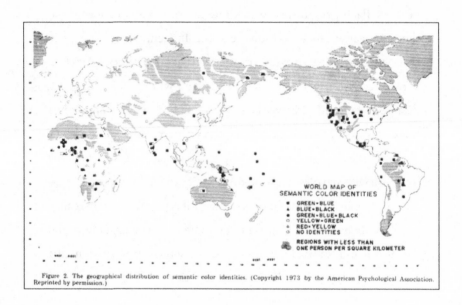

Figure 2. The geographical distribution of semantic color identities. (Copyright 1973 by the American Psychological Association. Reprinted by permission.)

World map identifying areas of the world with specific
"semantic color identities." Retrieved from Bornstein, 1975.

Mindfulness and *Kavanah*
Judaism's Ancient Tradition (13a)

אָמַר רַב יְהוּדָה: תֵּיתֵי לִי, דְּקַיֵּימִית עִיּוּן תְּפִלָּה

*Rav Yehuda said: May I receive my reward because
I fulfilled the obligation of kavana during prayer.*
— *Shabbos 118b*

Rabbi Moshe ben Nachman (Ramban), one of the great scholars in Jewish history, was ordered to participate in an event known as the "Disputation of Barcelona." In 1263, in front of the king and his royal court, Ramban debated with Pablo Christiani, a Jew who had converted to Christianity, regarding the authenticity of Christianity's claims about the Biblical support for their messiah. Despite, or perhaps because of, Ramban's successful defense of Judaism, Chrisitiani's supporters compelled Ramban to leave Spain. Although he was greatly pained to part from his family, Ramban fled to Israel to save his life.

Having left his family behind in Spain, Ramban composed a letter to his son, as explained in the *sefer Me'ulefes Sapirim*:

Ramban instructed his son to read the letter weekly and teach it to others, and become accustomed to recite it by heart, in order to train them in their youth to fear God (*yir'as shamayim*).

In absentia, Ramban wanted to impart the fundamental principles of how to achieve success in the service of God to his son and others who would read the letter, and as such, he selected the elements that he understood to be crucial to developing *yir'as shamayim*. Included in this list is eschewing anger, acting with great humility, and considering how one may practically apply principles of Torah learning to one's daily life. However, one instruction may seem surprising in its inclusion:

Cast external matters from your mind when you stand to pray; carefully prepare your heart in the presence of the Holy One. Purify your thoughts, and ponder your words before you utter them.[75]

From the inclusion of prayer in such a short letter, it is clear that Ramban regards prayer as a fundamental element of religious life, an idea which is not surprising. What is remarkable is what aspect of prayer he emphasizes. He does not ask his son to be cautious about praying with a *minyan*, nor does suggest that his son be zealous in keeping the proper *zemanim* (allotted times for prayer), even though both of those are requirements of *halachah*, and contribute to the power of the prayer that one recites. Instead, Ramban instructs his

---

75. Translation by Artscroll's *A Letter for the Ages*.

son to pray with, what would be called in contemporary language, mindfulness, which is defined as "bringing one's complete attention to the present experience on a moment-to-moment basis."[76] To pray with a *minyan*, to be exacting about the *zemanim*, even to be concerned with saying each word precisely, is insufficient to becoming a full *yarei shamayim*. If one wants to achieve this elevated distinction, one must practice mindful prayer, turning his thoughts away from worldly concerns and focusing solely on the experience and content of the prayers.

Despite the great important that Ramban placed on mindfulness during *tefillah*, he does not offer, at least in the letter, practical guidance for how to achieve such a lofty goal. How does one actually empty one's mind of external thoughts? How is it possible to focus only on the words and ideas of the prayers? What must a person do to prepare his heart to stand before God? Guidance from Chazal, as well as insight from contemporary psychological research and practice, may provide the skills to come closer to achieving this goal.

A Brief Overview of Mindfulness in Modern Practice

Mindfulness or meditative practice in the western world largely can be traced back to Buddhist traditions, and has gained enormous popularity following the introduction of its principles to lay people by a person named Satya Narayan Goenka, as noted in a *New York Times* obituary:[77]

76. Marlatt GA, Kristeller JL. Mindfulness and meditation. In: Miller WR, editor. *Integrating spirituality into treatment: Resources for practitioners.* Washington, D.C: American Psychological Association; 1999. pp. 67–84.

77. Retrieved from https://www.nytimes.com/2019/04/03/obitu-aries/sn-goenka-overlooked.html

"His legacy is enormous," said Sharon Salzberg, a meditation teacher who studied with Goenka in 1971. "If you have any interest in mindfulness today, it's thanks in part to Goenka."

Although most westerners who engage in mindfulness training are unaware of Goenka's name or role in introducing Buddhist thought to the western world, many of the leading practitioners of mindfulness in the psychological world attribute their understanding and teaching of mindfulness to Buddhist origins.[78] Buddhist mindfulness concepts are very present in the manuals for treatment modalities familiar to any student in mental health fields, such as Acceptance and Commitment Therapy (ACT) and Dialectical Behavioral Therapy (DBT), and it has increased in popularity among psychology practitioners, researchers, and training programs in the past twenty-plus years. Indeed, mindfulness training is considered an integral part of a wide variety of psychotherapeutic treatment for various conditions.[79]

While various interpretations and presentations of mindfulness exist, we will describe one approach that is commonly used in the

78. E.g., Kabat-Zinn, J. (1982). An outpatient program in behavioral medicine for chronic pain patients based on the practice of mindfulness meditation: Theoretical considerations and preliminary results. *General Hospital Psychiatry, 4*(1), 33-47.; Baer, R. A. (2003). Mindfulness training as a clinical intervention: A conceptual and empirical review. *Clinical Psychology: Science and Practice, 10*(2), 125-143. Linehan, M. (1993). *Skills training manual for treating borderline personality disorder* (Vol. 29). New York: Guilford Press.

79. Keng, S. L., Smoski, M. J., & Robins, C. J. (2011). Effects of mindfulness on psychological health: A review of empirical studies. *Clinical Psychology Review, 31*(6), 1041-1056.

psychological community. Dr. Marsha Linehan, the founder of DBT,[80] describes different types of mindfulness, which she defines generally as "the act of consciously focusing the mind in the present moment without judgment and without attachment to the moment." Mindfulness, as Dr. Linehan understands it, can be practiced anywhere, at any time, while engaging in any sort of activity. One specific type of mindfulness is call "meditation," which refers to the "practice of mindfulness while sitting or standing quietly for a period of time" (p. 151-152). She explains that two types of meditative mindfulness exercises may be performed. The first type is called "opening the mind," and it refers to observing or watching whatever comes into our awareness, be it thoughts, emotions, or physical sensations. The second type is known as "focusing the mind," and this refers to intentionally focusing on specific internal or external events. She adds that the latter type is often used as part of religious practice, either through mantras or visualizing religiously significant imagery.

Kavanah as Mindfulness

As we saw from Ramban, intentional thought and focus has long enjoyed great prominence in Torah and halachic sources, and it seems to date back at least to the days of the Tanna'im, nearly 2,000 years ago. In *halachah*, the closest word to "mindfulness" is *kavanah*, which has a variety of meanings depending on the context. *Kavanah* could refer to basic intent to perform a mitzvah, but that intent need not last any longer than the initiation of the mitzvah.[81] *Kavanah* can

---

80. Linehan, M. (2014). *DBT® skills training manual*. Guilford Publications.

81. See, for example, *Mishnah Berurah* 60:10.

also refer to understanding the basic meaning of words that said during *tefillah*; while attending to the meaning of the words extends throughout davening, it does not necessarily mean that other thoughts are absent.

For the purposes of this chapter, we will use the definition of *kavanah* for prayers as beautifully formulated by Rambam:

> Any prayer that is not [recited] with *kavanah* is not prayer. If one prays without *kavanah*, he must repeat his prayers with *kavanah*... What is meant by *kavanah*? *One should clear his mind from all thoughts and envision himself as standing before the Divine Presence.* Therefore, one must sit a short while before praying in order to focus his attention and then pray in a pleasant and supplicatory fashion (*Hilchos Tefillah u-Birkas Kohanim* 4:15-16).

In other words, consistent with Ramban, Rambam is instructing us that during our *tefillah*, we are to create a circumstance in which thoughts unrelated to prayer do not enter our minds. Mindfulness, or the ability to intentionally direct our thoughts, is thus a prerequisite for prayer, and, as Rambam rules, if we are not mindful, we do not fulfill our requirement to pray.[82]

Despite the similarities in the concept of mindfulness, this

---

82. Rav Chaim of Brisk (*Chidushei Rabbeinu Chaim HaLevi, Hilchos Tefillah* 4:1) clarifies that the type of *kavanah* that needs to be sustained throughout the *Amidah* is that the individual praying has *kavanah* that he is standing in prayer before Hashem; focus on the understanding of the specific words need only be during the first *berachah* to fulfill one's obligation to pray.

Rambam also highlights a crucial distinction between the goals of mindfulness for *tefillah* and the goals in many contemporary psychological practices. Mindfulness in *tefillah* is a means—albeit a necessary means—to an end of devoted prayer. For many in the world of psychology, achieving mindfulness, which represents "a state of psychological freedom,"[83] is an end in itself. Even Dr. Linehan's description of "focusing the mind" techniques in religious contexts assumes that the benefit of the practice is the achievement of mindfulness. Mindful living can be beneficial in many ways,[84] but from the perspective of contemporary psychology, mindfulness practice is in itself considered a valued goal. This inherent value of mindfulness is not reflected in halachic sources; instead, it is a state that forms the foundation for proper prayer or connection to the Divine. In this way there is a profound difference between the two schools of thought, even if there exists some overlap in both the problem being solved—the lack of focused attention of the mind—and the language being used to describe the state or process of mindfulness. In the tradition of *halachah*, learning to exert greater focus and control over one's mind is part of our devotion to God, and facilitates improved fulfillment of the *mitzvos*.

---

83. Martin, J. R. (1997). Mindfulness: A proposed common factor. *Journal of Psychotherapy Integration, 7*(4), 291.

84. Brown, K. W., & Ryan, R. M. (2003). The benefits of being present: Mindfulness and its role in psychological well-being. *Journal of Personality and Social Psychology, 84*(4), 822. Davis, D. M., & Hayes, J. A. (2011). What are the benefits of mindfulness? A practice review of psychotherapy-related research. *Psychotherapy, 48*(2), 198.

Practical Tips for Increasing Kavanah

My interest in this chapter is not to present a complete discussion of the principles of mindfulness or meditation, as the overlap between *halachah* and contemporary psychology is too broad a topic for this chapter.[85] However, my goal is to present two ideas from Chazal and contemporary psychological principles to help answer the question of *how* to achieve Ramban's instruction to "Cast external matters from your mind... Purify your thoughts, and ponder your words...."

Distracted Mind

As the purpose of mindfulness and *kavanah* is to develop the ability to purposefully direct one's thoughts toward *tefillah,* one might have reasoned that the external surroundings or environment should not be so important—perhaps the skills of achieving *kavanah* is meant to be practiced in all circumstances, so that one can be fully engaged in prayer no matter the surroundings. However, *halachah* recognizes some situations do not easily allow for sustained *kavanah*, which may be hinted at in the Torah itself. Bil'am, hoping to receive Divine prophecy, offered sacrifices with Balak, and then told Balak what would happen next (*Bamidbar* 23:3):

> Bil'am said to Balak, "Stand by your burnt-offering while I go; perhaps Hashem will happen toward me and show me something that I can tell you. He went alone [*shefi*].

---

85. For a recent book focusing on mindfulness in Jewish thought, see Epstein, B. (2018). *Living in the Presence: A Jewish Mindfulness Guide for Everyday Life.* Urim Publishing. Feiner, J. (2019). *In mindfulness: A Jewish approach.* Mosaica Press (2020).

This translation of the word *shefi* follows Rashi, based on the Targum Onkelos, who explains as follows: "The term denotes ease and quietness, that he was accompanied by nothing but silence."

In other words, Bil'am thought it was necessary to seclude himself in privacy, which apparently would help him receive Divine inspiration.

Although the story of Bil'am can be interpreted in different ways, it is clear that according to the Gemara, one should not pray in distracting environments, just as contemporary mindfulness exercises are typically conducted in quiet, calm settings, such as therapy rooms or yoga studios. For example, even though studying Torah prior to prayer is proper, the content should be straightforward so that the person's mind does not stray to the topic he was studying.[86] Rabbi Yaakov ben Asher, author of the *Arba'ah Turim* (known as *Tur*), cites several Amoraim who would not pray if they returned from a trip, had gotten upset, or were in a place with bothersome smells, all because they would be unable to sustain sufficient *kavanah* (98:2).[87]

The Sages also instructed people to avoid circumstances that may lead to anxiety or worry during their *tefillah,* as they will be unable to give their full attention to the prayers. For example, the *halachah* states that someone praying should be standing on solid ground, so that he will not worry that he may slip.[88] Also, the Gemara rules that during

---

86. Rashi, *Berachos* 31a, s.v. *halachah pesukah; Shulchan Aruch, Orach Chaim* 93:3.

87. This *halachah*, even if not practiced nowadays, leads to a remarkable conclusion regarding the centrality of *kavanah* to *tefillah.* According to one understanding of this approach, it is preferable to not pray at all than to pray without *kavanah.*

88. Rashi, *Berachos* 16a, s.v. *u-mispallelin be-rosh ha-zayis u-ve-rosh ha-ilan; Mishnah Berurah* 90:1.

prayer we should not carry expensive or delicate items, since concern about breaking them may impair our *kavanah*.[89]

Taken together, these *halachos* reflect the intuitive idea that distracting conditions lead people to become distracted. Although this may seem obvious, experience demonstrates that many people continue to introduce distractions into their surroundings, even during prayer, which has a deleterious effect on their ability to pray with optimal *kavanah*. For example, it is worth considering how the presence of cellphones in general, and smart phones in particular, relates to the requirement of achieving and maintaining *kavanah*.[90] Of course, it seems unfair to fellow congregants for a person to bring a phone that may ring or vibrate loudly and will disturb others' prayers. Similarly, if a person has the screen visible to openly display incoming calls or messages, he is, by definition, not fully focused on *tefillah*. However, even if it is silently on the table or on vibrate in one's pocket, modern research provides additional reasons to be cautious of bringing a phone into *shul*. In several recent studies[91] focusing on college students, researchers found that physical proximity to one's cell phone, even if the person did not actively use the phone, diminished various aspects of their cognitive functioning:[92]

89. *Berachos* 23b, see Rashi and Rabbeinu Yonah there.
90. See *Shu"t Le-horos Nasan* 11:9 for a consideration of various halachic factors.
91. E.g., Thornton, B., Faires, A., Robbins, M., & Rollins, E. (2014). The mere presence of a cell phone may be distracting. *Social Psychology, 45*(6), 479-488.
92 Ward, A. F., Duke, K., Gneezy, A., & Bos, M. W. (2017). Brain drain: The mere presence of one's own smartphone reduces available cognitive capacity. *Journal of the Association for Consumer Research, 2*(2), 140-154.

...even when people are successful at maintaining sustained attention—as when avoiding the temptation to check their phones—the mere presence of these devices reduces available cognitive capacity.

As such, it would seem that it is not simply using the phone or having the phone active that would diminish one's ability to have *kavanah*, but even having the phone present in *shul* may serve as a distraction.

Finally, when it comes to distractions to *kavanah*, if we are taking *tefillah* seriously, we must each consider for ourselves what types activities or items enhance or diminish our mindfulness in prayer. What for some people may be helpful is for others a terrible impediment to concentration. As such, in order to fulfill Ramban's instruction, a first step is to examine for oneself what increases or decreases distractions, and to take actions to implement those discoveries into his *tefillah*.

Posture

The use of posture is one way to create an environment in which we can control our thoughts in our desired direction. Variants of the sitting position—lotus position on the floor, sitting on a pillow, kneeling, or seated on a chair—are common in mindfulness exercises, and sitting meditations have even been formally incorporated into psychotherapeutic interventions, such as Mindfulness Based Stress Reduction (MBSR).

Although the predominant posture for mindfulness in contemporary practice is sitting, experts have also noted the benefit of other postures in mindfulness practice. Take, for example, Dr. Linehan's definition of "meditation" (p. 46):[93]

Meditation is practicing mindfulness and mindfulness skills while sitting, standing, or lying quietly for a predetermined period of time.

As she highlights, assuming a posture—be it sitting, standing, or reclining—is an integral part of mindfulness practice; similarly, halachah also recognizes that these postures may be conducive for kavanah, and each are identified in various contexts as contributing to enhanced focus for prayer.

Sitting

The Gemara (Berachos 51b) records the following halachah: "In all these cases [i.e., one who is eating while walking, standing, sitting, or reclining], one should sit and recite the birkas ha-mazon [grace after meals]." Although the Gemara does not provide an explanation for this ruling, Rabbi Asher ben Yechiel (Rosh) seems to interpret the reasoning behind this halachah as an issue of kavanah; as a result, he adds that those who are traveling would preferably not stop if stopping to sit would distract their focus even more than if they were to continue walking.[94] Tur (Orach Chaim 183:9), presumably based on the commentary of Rosh, adds this reasoning explicitly, stating that one should sit so that "he may have better kavanah."

---

93. Linehan, M. (2014). DBT® Skills Training Handouts and Worksheets. Guilford Publications.

94. See commentators on the Talmud Yerushalmi (Berachos 7:5), who provide an alternate explanation based on a variant text.

Although the *Amidah* itself must be said standing, some commentators argue that Rambam specifically refers to "sitting" prior to *tefillah* as preparation for prayer while one clears his mind of extraneous thoughts, as the *Divrei Chamudos* writes:[95]

> That which he said "to sit" refers specifically to sitting, and not just to taking pause while standing; this is for good reason, as certainly through sitting his mind is more at ease to have *kavanah* for what he wants.

Moreover, Rambam implies that one should specifically sit for *Ashrei* prior to *Minchah*,[96] and Rav Chaim of Brisk is quoted[97] as explaining that this requirement to sit is part of the necessary preparations for *tefillah*.[98]

---

95. Commentator on Rosh, *Berachos* 5:37.
96. *Hilchos Tefillah u-Birkas Kohanim* 9:8.
97. See Frankel's *Sefer Ha-Mafteach* on the preceding *halachah*.
98. It is worth considering that sitting in *halachah* includes the various ways of sitting used in contemporary mindfulness practice. Of course, sitting on some type of chair is a typical form of sitting, emerging from a Biblical source (*Vayikra* 15:4). However, other sources suggest that sitting on the floor is also referred to as sitting. For example, the Mishnah in *Zevachim* (2:1) discusses disqualifying factors for the *kabbalas ha-dam* of a sacrifice: "All sacrifices whose blood was caught...[while] sitting, [or while] standing on utensils or on an animal or on his fellow's feet, are disqualified." This "sitting" appears to refer to being seated on the ground and not on a chair, as the Gemara there explains regarding "standing on a utensil"— even if one foot is on the ground—that the test of whether he is considered on a utensil is whether he would still be able to stand if the utensil were pulled away. If sitting referred to sitting on a chair,

Similarly, the Gemara in *Megillah* (21a) discusses what posture Moshe Rabbeinu assumed while both receiving the Torah on Har Sinai, as well as when he was reviewing the material that he had learned. The final view presented there states: "Rava said, the easy things he learned standing, while the hard ones he learned sitting." The commentators assume that the standing position is preferable to display *kavod* (honor), and, as Rashi writes, simpler topics may be understood quickly even in a standing position; however, the need to focus on more difficult topics necessitated Moshe sitting,[99] indicating that a sitting posture provides an enhanced ability for sustained attention.

Standing

The emphasis on sitting to enhance *kavanah* seems not to be accepted universally. For example, the Gemara (*Berachos* 30a) discusses the changes certain Sages made to their davening times to accommodate other items in their daily schedules. The Gemara records the practice of Rav Ashi when he would start his lecture in the early morning:

---

the kohen would be disqualified because he would be considered on a utensil; thus, it seems that "sitting" refers to being on the ground. In other places (e.g., *Megillah* 21a), sitting clearly is less specific, and refers to either on a mat/chair, or on the ground.

99. Notably, some Rishonim appear to argue with the assertion that sitting enhances *kavanah*; instead, as Rivash (ch. 412) writes: "And that which the *tzibbur* has the custom to sit [for *nefilas apayim*] is consistent with their custom to sit for all of their *tefillos* and *berachos*, in order not to be too great of a disturbance [*tircha*]— that is, except for the *Amidah*."

Rav Ashi used to say the *tefillah* while still with the congregation sitting[100] and when he returned home he used to say it again standing.

Rashi, in explaining this passage, adds several words not found in the comments of other Rishonim: "...and when [Rav Ashi] would return home, he would pray again standing *le-chavein es libbo* (in order to have *kavanah*).

Later authorities do not highlight these additional words in Rashi. Nevertheless, it seems that Rashi is addressing what added benefit Rav Ashi gains by praying again if he fulfilled his obligation with the *tefillah* while seated. Apparently, Rashi understood that the standing posture allows for greater *kavanah* than does the seated posture, which would justify Rav Ashi's repetition of the *Amidah*.

Nefilas Apayim

According to *Tur* (*Orach Chaim* 131), the Torah's description of three separate postures practiced by Moshe on Har Sinai—sitting, standing, and *Nefilas Apayim*[101]—was associated with different aspects of *kavanah*. Specifically regarding *Nefilas Apayim*, *Tur* writes that the practice prostrating face-down is meant to mirror

---

100. As Rashi explains, in those times, the lecturer delivered his message to an intermediary, the *meturgeman*, who would then repeat the information to the students in the study hall. Rav Ashi would give a large amount of information allowing him sufficient time to recite the *Amidah*.

101. Various customs regarding how to fulfill *Nefilas Apayim* have emerged over the generations, including some type of bowing, sitting, or standing.

the position described in the Torah as Moshe prayed on behalf of the Jewish people after the sin of the golden calf: "I threw myself down before Hashem for the forty days and the forty nights that I threw myself down, for Hashem had intended to destroy you." Based on this approach, that we practice *Nefilas Apayim* simply to mirror Moshe's precedence, the *Nefilas Apayim* posture is not necessarily meant to enhance *kavanah,* and according to Rabbi Yitzchak bar Sheshes (Rivash) (*teshuvah* 412) it is not part of the obligation of *tefillah.* Nevertheless, the commentators seem to agree that *Nefilas Apayim* implies increased intensity of supplication (Rambam, *Hilchos Tefillah* 5:15); as such, assuming this posture may help a person achieve higher levels of *kavanah* in some circumstances.

From the discussion of these various postures, it seems that there is not universal agreement about which posture is considered best for one's *kavanah.* Of course, regarding *tefillah, keriyas Shema, birkas ha-mazon,* and other activities that require concentration, *kavanah* may not be the determining factor in what type of posture a person is meant to maintain, and *halachah* may demand a person assume a specific posture for reasons independent of *kavanah.* Nevertheless, as we have seen, the Gemara, Rishonim, and contemporary mindfulness experts recognize that one's physical posture is an integral feature of focusing one's mind, and, as such, deserves self-reflection regarding what type of posture helps each person achieve better *kavanah.*

Lesson for Today

Despite the emphasis on the importance of developing the ability to focus mindfully on one's *tefillah,* Chazal also recognized that such a lofty level of focus is not easily attainable. Even the Sages of the Talmud themselves asserted their difficulty maintaining complete *kavanah* throughout the entire *Amidah* (silent devotion):

> Rav Chiya the Great said, "In all my days I never concentrated [without any extraneous thought]. One time I wanted to concentrate and I meditated. And I said to myself, 'Who goes up first before the king? The *Arkafta* or the Exilarch?'" Shmuel said, "I count the birds." Rav Bun bar Chiya said, "I count rows of bricks." Said Rabbi Matna, "I consider myself lucky. For when I reach the Thanksgiving blessing [*Modim*], I bow instinctively" (Talmud Yerushalmi, *Berachos* 2:4).[102]

In other words, despite these Rabbis' elevated spiritual achievements and mental abilities, they too struggled to maintain the level of *kavanah* that they expected from themselves. This challenge is one that is recognized by more recent Torah scholars:

> However, it is true that our sins take away goodness from us... to the point that we are unable to direct our thoughts and serve our Creator with full and pure service... and daily stressors and circumstances cloud our thinking.... Nevertheless, we will be held accountable for not trying [to achieve *kavanah*] with great strength, and that which

102. See Gra, *Orach Chayim* 101:3, who seems to take these comments at face value, that the Rabbis expressed difficulty with *kavanah*. However, other commentators take the comments less literally; see, for example, *Chasam Sofer* on this passage in the Talmud Yerushalmi.

we were able to do, we did not do… (*Peleh Yoetz,* chapter on *kavanah*).

In this passage, the *Peleh Yoetz* acknowledges that, as humans with human failings, complete focus and *kavanah* may be an unrealistic goal; despite that reality, and as with other aspects of our spiritual life, the fact that we cannot achieve perfection does not absolve us from putting in effort to achieve greater heights.

The struggle to achieve and maintain mindfulness has spanned thousands of years, and has been experienced by scholars and laypeople alike across many cultures. The Talmudic tradition offers powerful lessons into the need to develop and improve upon the ability to intentionally focus one's mind, which is part of one's optimal service of God. Above, I have described two primary aspects that emerge from Chazal—removing distractions, and assuming postures that are conducive of mindfulness—of *how* a person may obtain these skills, which can help someone praying to fulfil the instructions of Ramban regarding how he should pray. Both Jew and gentile alike would benefit from following the practical guidance of these ancient and well-tested traditions to optimize their experience of *kavanah* and mindfulness.

The Path of Least Resistance
Using Deterrence to Influence Behavior (22a)

אָמְרָה לוֹ רֵיקָא! יֵשׁ לְךָ אַרְבָּעִים סְאָה שֶׁאַתָּה טוֹבֵל בָּהֶן!? מִיָּד פֵּירַשׁ

"Good-for-nothing! Do you have forty se'ah in which to immerse yourself afterwards? He immediately desisted."

In 1994, the Surgeon General issued a report focusing on preventing youth from smoking tobacco products. Since then, researchers in a variety of fields have developed and evaluated various methods aimed at ways to prevent or deter people from smoking tobacco.[103] There was a general recognition that simply having laws on the books prohibiting smoking was insufficient, and law enforcement lacked the enormous amount of resources that would be necessary to solve this problem through policing alone. As a result, in addition to media campaigns, school-based, and family-based interventions, increasing attention was given to deterring smoking through changes to the physical environment.

One type of strategy involved instituting "smoke-free zones," including workplaces, restaurants, parks, or other areas that had previously been open to people smoking cigarettes. Although these

---

103. US Department of Health and Human Services. (2012). Preventing tobacco use among youth and young adults: a report of the Surgeon General. 2012. Washington, DC: *US Department of Health and Human Services.*

laws, enacted at the state and local levels, did not directly address access to cigarettes, a recent longitudinal study found that adopting smoke-free workplaces had an effect reducing the initiation of smoking similar to the effect of adoption a cigarette tax of over $1.50 per pack.[104]

How are we to understand this deterrence effect caused by creating smoke-free zones? One explanation, drawn from the fields of criminology and behavioral economics, could be that the increase in perceived effort involved in a behavior leads to a reduction in that behavior.[105] For example, the perception that a smoke-free workplace will require increased effort, and potentially some level of annoyance, may lead a smoker to use cigarettes less often, and may lead non-smokers to refrain from starting in the first place. This principle can be summed up in the following paragraph:

> We know that criminal and deviant acts have something in common because participation in any one of them predicts participation in all of the others.... People who rob and steal are more likely than people who do not rob and steal to smoke and drink, use illegal drugs, break into houses, and cheat on tests. What do robbery, theft, burglary, cheating, truancy, and drug use (and the many forms of criminal and deviant behavior not listed) have in common? They are all quick and easy ways of getting what one wants.[106]

104. Song, A. V., Dutra, L. M., Neilands, T. B., & Glantz, S. A. (2015). Association of smoke-free laws with lower percentages of new and current smokers among adolescents and young adults: an 11-year longitudinal study. *JAMA Pediatrics, 169*(9), e152285-e152285.

105. E.g., Clarke, R. V. G. (Ed.). (1997). *Situational crime prevention.* Monsey, NY: Criminal Justice Press. p. 225-256.

106. Cited in Nagin, D. S., & Pogarsky, G. (2003). An experimental investigation of deterrence: Cheating, self-serving bias, and impulsivity. *Criminology, 41*(1), 167-194.

In other words, if acting in a deviant way cannot be done as easily on impulse, and more effort is required, the undesired act will likely be less common.

Chazal were aware that increased effort required to perform an act will lead to the act to be less common, as shown regarding the proper height of Chanukah candles for shopkeepers lighting in the public domain. The Gemara suggests one reason that the shopkeeper may not be required to lift his candles above the level of people and animals walking through the market is because "if you burden him excessively, he will come to refrain from performing the mitzvah." The Rabbis reasoned that the minimal elevation of risk of monetary damages does not outweigh the likely scenario that shopkeepers would refrain from lighting candles altogether (*Shabbos* 21b).

Most of the psychological literature has focused on the effects of increased effort *prior* to the undesired behavior, or, alternatively, on the threat and enforcement of punishments for the misdeed that come after the violation of a certain law. Less research has examined whether increased effort following the indiscretion may also serve as a deterrence, although a passage in the Gemara offers an insight from Chazal that can shed light onto this question.

One of the ten enactments attributed to Ezra is the requirement for someone who sees a seminal emission, which brings about the *tum'ah* (ritual impurity) of a *ba'al keri*, to immerse in water in order to study of Torah (*Bava Kamma* 82b). The Gemara discusses various laws pertaining to this Rabbinic decree, and two primary disagreements emerge regarding a *ba'al keri* (*Berachos* 22):

1. What are the prohibited activities for a *ba'al keri*, such as *tefillah* or Torah study?

2. How does one restore his status of *taharah* (ritual purity) so that he may resume the prohibited activities: through immersion in a *mikveh* of forty *se'ah* rain water, or, alternatively, by pouring nine *kav* of water of one's head?

In the course of presenting the views of various Sages, the Gemara is curious why some people immerse in the morning in a full *mikveh* with forty *se'ah* of water, even though, according to the opinion at this stage of the Gemara, the letter of the law only requires pouring water over one's head.

One Sage seems to reply that this stringency is a positive one, as there were unintended benefits to requiring full immersion:

> [Regarding the requirement of forty *se'ah*], Rabbi Chanina said: They established a massive fence [preventing one from sinning], as it was taught in a *baraisa*: there was an incident involving one who solicited a woman to commit a sinful act. She said to him: Good-for-nothing! Do you have forty *se'ah* in which to immerse yourself afterwards? He immediately desisted.

Rabbi Chanina is not arguing that the purpose of the Rabbinic requirement to immerse is in order to add an additional layer of protection against those who intend to engage in inappropriate sexual relationships. Instead, it appears that Rabbi Chanina is highlighting an additional, indirect benefit of the *takkanah* (rabbinic enactment), namely that the requirement to find forty *se'ah* in order to return to Torah study or prayer creates a deterrence against impulsively engaging in sinful behavior.

Intuitively, one might assume that such a deterrent would only work against minor impulses, and that deterrence through increased effort would not have an effect on strong impulses. As I will show below, this does not seem to be the opinion of the Sages, as demonstrated by how the Gemara views sexual transgressions. The Gemara (*Sanhedrin* 26b) considers the status of people who violate various types sins as they relate to giving testimony. Rabbi Nachman asserts that even though typically someone who violates Torah law may not be accepted as a valid witness, someone who is *chashud al arayos*—suspected of engaging in illicit sexual relations—is still accepted for most testimonies. Tosafos there ask why such a person is any different than those who violate other transgressions, such as eating non-kosher meat lustfully, which do invalidate a person from being a viable witness. In his second answer, Tosafos writes:

> This is a case of *yitzro tokfo* ("he was overcome by desire"), in contrast to the case of non-kosher meat... which does not involve *yitzro tokfo* to the same extent as illicit sexual relationships.

Tosafos is arguing that because sexual desire is so strong, just because a person would violate a sexual prohibition does not mean he will necessarily violate the prohibition of testifying falsely for monetary gain. In other words, the Gemara is recognizing that some people will succumb to an impulsive urge, and this inability to overcome this impulse does not necessarily reflect on his ability to overcome the impulse to testify falsely for his own benefit. With this in mind, the insight of Rabbi Chanina's statement in *Berachos* is even more remarkable: an action which carries with it such a strong urge may be deterred by requiring extra effort to purify afterwards![107]

Rabbi Chanina's observation supports the contemporary research on deterrence, that adding additional effort to committing a deviant act may serve to prevent a person from acting on the impulse for the deviancy. Of course, this requirement clearly does not stop everyone from sinning, just as a tax increase of $1.50 does not stop everyone from smoking cigarettes; however, Rabbi Chanina is pointing to the power of this additional effort to create a deterrence against impulsive, deviant behavior. He also provides a valuable insight that extends the application of this principle: not only might additional effort *prior* to committing the act provide deterrence, but the requirement of extra effort *following* the act may also be an effective deterrent.

Deterrence of Inclement Weather

Contemporary literature focusing on a different type of deterrence, namely inclement weather or climate, may also provide an explanation for a *halachah* related to the establishment of *kedushah* (holiness) in Yerushalayim, and perhaps even the *Beis Ha-Mikdash* itself.[108] In the

---

107. One might ask the question regarding whether it is reasonable to think, from the perspective of religious observance, that a person who would engage in sinful sexual relations would also be careful to immerse in a *mikveh* following these relations. See the Gemara (*Shabbos* 127b) for a story that suggests a person would, indeed, be capable of both illicit sexual relations and commitment to immersing.

108. I am not referring to the large-scale impact of weather or climate, such as the relationship between weather and crime in the research

early 2000's, before early voting composed a substantial proportion of voters, researchers examined the role of inclement weather in voter participation in national elections. This study of every county in the United States found that on average, each inch of rain was associated with a decline in voter rates of around 1%, and each inch of snow associated with a decline of roughly 0.5%.[109] As they note, these percentages may have been enough to swing elections. As it relates to deterrence, the important finding of this study is that even relatively minor inconveniences, such as an inch of rain, can have a direct deterrence effect on the behavior of people who likely would have voted otherwise.

This insight about climate as a possible deterrent may help explain a Talmudic passage. As background, the Mishnah (*Keilim* 1:6-9) describes ten levels of *kedushah* related to one's location in the Land of Israel. Each level of *kedushah* is associated with additional restrictions regarding who may enter that place or what activities are permitted in that place. For example, outside the

---

literature (e.g., Cohn, E. G. (1990). Weather and crime. *The British Journal of Criminology*, 30(1), 51-64.); or, within *halachah*, the many places that the potential interference of rain for those who are oleh la-regel is cause for Rabbinic concern. I am also not discussing Chazal's use of sun and shade to influence a behavior, as Rav Sheshes did (*Shabbos* 119a), or the recognition that weather may influence certain generic behaviors, such as the assumption that a cold or hot day may lead a person to not go for a walk on Shabbos (*Eiruvin* 52a and Rashi 51b). Instead, my focus is specifically the power of inclement weather to deter specific desirable behaviors, both in Chazal and in contemporary research.

109. Gomez, B. T., Hansford, T. G., & Krause, G. A. (2007). The Republicans should pray for rain: Weather, turnout, and voting in US presidential elections. *The Journal of Politics*, 69(3), 649-663.

walls of Yerushalayim, one may not eat certain sanctified foods, such as *kodshim kalim* (lower-level sacrificial meat) or *ma'aser sheini* (the second tithe). The next level of *kedusha* is within the walls of the Temple Mount, where people with various types of *tum'ah* are prohibited from entering. Both of these levels of *kedushah* have relevance for someone with the designation of a *metzora* (someone who has *tzara'as*, see *Vayikra 13*). The *metzora* may not dwell within the walls of the city, and he is also prohibited from entering the Temple Mount. Also of note, part of the final stage of purification for a *metzora* includes bringing a sacrifice to the Temple and having blood from the sacrifice sprinkled upon him; until he completes this process, he can transmit *tum'ah* to others.

While there is a clear distinction between inside and outside these walls of either Yerushalayim or the Temple Mount, the Gemara discusses the question of whether the thickness of a wall is considered to have the level of *kedushah* of the area inside the wall or outside the wall (*Pesachim* 85b). The relevance of this question is whether someone standing on the threshold is considered in the area of higher *kedushah*—with all the applicable restrictions or permissions—or is considered to be in the area of lower *kedushah*. Even though the Gemara asserts that generally the thickness of walls of the Temple courtyard contain the *kedushah* of the internal area, one gate—Sha'ar Nikanor—has a different law, as do the walls around Yerushalayim; in the case of Sha'ar Nikanor and Yerushalayim the threshold is considered outside the Temple Mount or city, respectively, and thus given the lower level of sanctity. The Gemara cites two similar, but not identical, statements of Rabbi Shmuel bar Yitzchak to explain why the thickness of the walls of Yerushalayim, as well as Sha'ar Nikanor, were not given the higher level of sanctity. Regarding the walls of Yerushalayim, the Gemara explains:

As Rabbi Shmuel bar Rav Yitzchak said: For what reason were the insides of the gates of Jerusalem not sanctified? Because *metzora'im* protect themselves under them; in the sun they protect themselves from the sun and in the rain they protect themselves from the rain.

Regarding Sha'ar Nikanor, the following explanation is given:

Rabbi Shmuel bar Rav Yitzchak said: For what reason was the inside of Sha'ar Nikanor not sanctified with the sanctity of the Temple courtyard? It is because metzora'im would stand there and insert their thumbs into the courtyard [so that the blood of the offerings could be sprinkled on them, which would allow them to be purified].

Tosafos (*Yevamos* 7b, s.v. *zeh nichnas*) wonders why this gate needed to have a different law to the rest—after all, if the thickness of walls of Sha'ar Nikanor were sanctified, the *metzora'im* could simply stand outside the walls and stick their hands into Sha'ar Nikanor to fulfil their needs. Rabbeinu Tam offers an explanation similar to the explanation in *Pesachim* for the law regarding the walls of Yerushalayim, with an addition of a unique phrase:

It was so because of the *takkanas ha-metzora'im* [institution of the Rabbinic ordinance for the *metzora'im*] that they should stand there, so that they should be protected in the sun from the sun, and be protected from the rain in the rain.

According to a basic reading of Rabbeinu Tam's answer, Sha'ar Nikanor and the walls of Yerushalayim have the same *halachah* is for the same reason—those with *tzara'as* can make use of the coverage provided by the gateway to protect them from the elements. However, two questions can be asked regarding this explanation of Rabbeinu Tam's position. First, if the reasons for the *halachah* are the same, why would Rabbi Shmuel bar Rav Yitzchak provide two separate explanations? Second, why would we make a special dispensation for the *metzora'im* coming to be purified, whose discomfort may last all of a half-hour while the ritual is performed?

Applying the principle observed in contemporary times regarding the role of climate and deterrence of desired behavior, a different explanation of Rabbeinu Tam's comment might be suggested. The *metzora* would have completed an extended and gruelling process of excommunication and healing, and he would be eager to return to normal communal life. However, consider his attitude if he wakes up on the morning of the eighth day of his purification process to rain clouds overhead, or a bright, summer sun beating down on his head from above. While many *metzora'im* would complete the purification process and overcome the urge to stay home, it is not hard to imagine some deciding against standing in the harsh elements, thereby foregoing the final, necessary step to becoming *tahor*.

In other words, perhaps Chazal recognized that the harsh elements would be a deterrent against the *metzora'im* completing their purification, which would have a profound impact on the larger society. The *metzora* would be presumed by others to be pure, and he would return to normal life and making everything *tamei* in the process. By not sanctifying the thickness of the walls, Chazal were removing a potential deterrent and increasing the odds that the *metzora* will follow through on the purification ritual.

This explanation may be hinted to by Rabbeinu Tam's usage of the unique term, *takkanas metzora'im*, which, to my knowledge, is not used anywhere else in Rabbinic literature. It is reminiscent of the term *takkanas ha-shavim*, which includes various laws and leniencies that Chazal instituted in order to encourage people to do *teshuvah* after stealing property. For example, if a thief stole a beam and used it to build a house, by the letter of the law he should disassemble the wall and return the original beam he stole. However, the Mishnah (*Gittin* 55a) rules that instead of knocking down the wall to return the beam, the repentant thief may return the value of the beam instead. Rashi explains:

> For if you would require him to knock down his building and return the beam itself, he would be prevented from doing *teshuvah*.

The Sages recognized that requiring this great effort, at a loss of time and money to the thief, would discourage and deter a thief from doing *teshuvah* and returning anything; as a result, they instituted this leniency that he return the value of the beam, and not the actual beam.

If this reading of Rabbeinu Tam is correct, we can address the two questions posed above. The first question was why would Rabbi Shmuel bar Rav Yitzchak give two different answers if he really meant the same thing by both. According to our current approach, the two answers are very different, even if Rabbeinu Tam uses similar language. Regarding the walls of Yerushalayim, it would be unreasonably cruel to force them to brave the sun and rain outside the city gates for an extended period of time of days and weeks; the reason we would make this accommodation is out of compassion for the *metzora's* suffering. However, regarding Sha'ar Nikanor, it is because we need him to "stand there and insert his thumb into the courtyard," and if it too uncomfortable, he may simply not show up.

If this reading is correct, this discussion about deterrence related to inclement weather is an excellent example of how both the wisdom of Chazal and the analysis of contemporary science complement one another. Modern scientists were not the first to discover how minor annoyances of the weather may deter certain positive behaviors; indeed, the recognition of this reality may date back to at least the building of the Second Temple nearly 2,500 years ago! However, without the direct research revealing the capacity of climate or weather to influence behavior, the subtlety and nuance of Rabbeinu Tam's answer, and reinterpretation of Rabbi Shmuel bar Rav Yitzchak's answer, may not have been noticed.

Lesson for Today

The examples of deterrence presented above are somewhat opposite. In the first instance, Chazal recognized the power of extra effort to deter someone from sinning; in the second instance, Chazal saw that one may be deterred from a positive action that we would want him to perform. In both cases, it is remarkable that the deterring factor is a relatively minor extra step, yet the added exertion necessary can have a profound effect on a person's behavior.

Applying principles of deterrence can also be useful interventions in how we encourage ourselves and our children to act in more desirable ways, and it is important to identify deterrents that may be present that discourage us from behaving in accordance with our more lofty values. In my clinical practice, an example for which deterrence may be especially relevant is regarding electronics for ourselves and our children. Many people struggle with their usage of phones, computers, or some devices, spending more time on these devices than they would like, or accessing materials that go against their religious or spiritual values. Of course, no single strategy for changing this behavior will work for everyone, but it is worth considering whether the principles of deterrence may be useful. Would increasing the effort involved in using the devices decrease their usage? For example, if every time we were going to use an electronic device we would have to ask someone else for its location or passcode, there is no doubt it would create a situation of deterrence from usage. Of course, just as deterrence in the Gemara and the scientific literature does not solve every problem or create a fool-proof solution, nor does deterrence necessarily prevent us from doing positive things that we would want. Nevertheless, the better we can be at becoming aware of the deterring elements in our lives, the greater ability we can have to live according to the choices that we want to make.

Somebody to Lean On
Bullying and the Role of the Defender (23a)

וְאָמְרָה רָאוּ מַה נָתַן לִי פְּלוֹנִי בִּשְׂכָרִי!

כֵּיוָן שֶׁשָׁמַע אוֹתוֹ תַּלְמִיד כָּךְ עָלָה לְרֹאשׁ הַגַּג וְנָפַל וָמֵת

And she said "See what so-and-so gave me as payment!"
When the student heard this, he climbed to the roof, fell off, and died.

Jamel Myles was bullied by schoolmates throughout his third grade. His mother, Leia Pierce, frequently spoke with teachers and administrators to address her son's experience of being victimized by classmates, with the hopes that they might be able to reduce or eliminate the bullying of her son. During the summer between 3rd and 4th grade, Jamel told his mother that he was gay, and that he wanted to start dressing in a more feminine way. He also wanted to tell his classmates. Ms. Pierce told a local paper: "My son told my oldest daughter the kids at school told him to kill himself. I'm just sad he didn't come to me…. I'm so upset that he thought that was his option."[110]

This tragic story, unfortunately, is not unique. In recent years,

---

110. https://kdvr.com/2018/08/26/mom-says-denver-boy-killed-himself-after-being-bullied-at-school/.

administrators, teachers, and parents have become increasingly aware of the problem of bullying, which is typically defined as "aggressive behavior, in which an individual or a group of individuals repeatedly attacks, humiliates, and/or excludes a relatively powerless person."[111] In addition to the miserable experience of being a victim of bullying, negative effects do not necessarily stop when the bullying ends. A prospective study of children suggests a causal relationship between being bullied in childhood with emotional problems in adolescence,[112] and may be a risk factor for depression later in life.[113] Perhaps the most distressing effect of bullying is its apparent relationship with suicidality,[114] a heartbreaking outcome as shown by the story of

111. Salmivalli, C. (2010). Bullying and the peer group: A review. *Aggression and Violent Behavior, 15*(2), 112-120.

112 Bond, L., Carlin, J. B., Thomas, L., Rubin, K., & Patton, G. (2001). Does bullying cause emotional problems? A prospective study of young teenagers. *British Medical Journal, 323*(7311), 480-484.

113. Ttofi, M. M., Farrington, D. P., Lösel, F., & Loeber, R. (2011). Do the victims of school bullies tend to become depressed later in life? A systematic review and meta-analysis of longitudinal studies. *Journal of Aggression, Conflict and Peace Research, 3*(2), 63-73.

114. E.g., Klomek, A. B., Marrocco, F., Kleinman, M., Schonfeld, I. S., & Gould, M. S. (2007). Bullying, depression, and suicidality in adolescents. *Journal of the American Academy of Child & Adolescent Psychiatry, 46*(1), 40-49.; Klomek, A. B., Sourander, A., & Gould, M. (2010). The association of suicide and bullying in childhood to young adulthood: A review of cross-sectional and longitudinal research findings. *The Canadian Journal of Psychiatry, 55*(5), 282-288. Kim, Y. S., & Leventhal, B. (2008). Bullying and suicide. A review. *International Journal of Adolescent Medicine and Health, 20*(2), 133-154. Hinduja, S., & Patchin, J. W. (2010). Bullying, cyberbullying, and suicide. *Archives of Suicide Research, 14*(3), 206-221.

young Jamel. Although it is not entirely clear from scientific research *why* suicidality may result from bullying,[115] it is an association that seems to have been noted by Chazal, as well. I will present two instances, one from the gemara and one from Tanach, of disastrous consequences related to the harsh treatment of others, and consider how contemporary perspectives on bullying relate to the cases in Torah literature. In particular, I will focus on the role of onlookers who observe the harsh treatment, and how their stance toward the offender or the victims may affect the outcome of the situation.

The Story of False Accusations

In the times of the Gemara, the practice was for men to wear *tefillin* (phylacteries) all day, not only during the morning prayer service (as the practice is nowadays). As *tefillin* are considered *tashmishei kedushah* [articles associated with the sanctity of God's name] (*Megillah* 26b), there are significant restrictions regarding how someone must treat the *tefillin* or act while donning them. An obvious problem faced by people in the times of Chazal was what to do with the *tefillin* when one was using the toilet, either by urination or defecation, as the level of tefillin's *kedushah* leads to a prohibition to bring them into a bathroom. In those days, people would relieve themselves in outdoor, enwalled locations. After discussing various opinions of the proper practice, the Gemara (*Berachos* 23a) cites a progression of views regarding what one should do with the *tefillin*. At one point, the ruling was that one should remove them outside the toilet, and place them in a crevice in the wall prior to entering.

---

115. Espelage, D. L., & Holt, M. K. (2013). Suicidal ideation and school bullying experiences after controlling for depression and delinquency. *Journal of Adolescent Health, 53*(1), S27-S31.

However, due to the following story, Chazal ruled that it is preferable to hold the *tefillin* in one's hand, and cover them with his garment:

> A student placed his phylacteries in the holes adjacent to the public domain, and a prostitute passed by and took the phylacteries. She came to the study hall and said: See what so-and-so gave me as my payment! When that student heard this, he ascended to the rooftop and fell and died. At that moment they instituted that one should hold them with his garment and in his hand and enter to avoid situations of that kind.[116]

On the one hand, this act of humiliation was not a repeated event, and as such is not identical to other instances of bullying; nevertheless, what this prostitute did was certainly an aggressive behavior aimed at humiliating a relatively powerless individual, which is, at its core, what bullying is all about.

Although the commentators do not provide much elaboration regarding this story, a close examination of the sequence of events may shed light on important implications of this story. It appears that the prostitute must have seen the student remove his *tefillin* and place them into the crevice of the wall—otherwise, how would she have known to whom the *tefillin* belonged—and she seized the opportunity to humiliate him. What chaos must have ensued as she

---

116. This is similar to the *gezeirah* quoted in *Shabbos* 60a. Just as here Chazal made a ruling based on an impulsive reaction that turned tragic, there they outlawed wearing cleats on Shabbos due to a case where people trampled others with cleats to escape a feared attack by their oppressors.

entered the study hall and made the announcement; there she was, a prostitute publicly claiming to have been patronized by a Rabbinic scholar she could identify by name, and she had his *tefillin* to prove it!

One wonders: What did the other students think, and what was their reaction? Perhaps the next line of the story gives an indication: "When that student heard this." What did he hear and from whom? Apparently, he was not in the *beis midrash* (study hall) when the prostitute made her shocking claim. One can imagine that when he exited the toilet and noticed his *tefillin* missing, he was upset and frustrated that someone seemed to have stolen them. In this state of being distressed and saddened, he headed back toward the study hall, perhaps to make an announcement himself to see if anyone has his *tefillin*. He may already be feeling some level of embarrassment, as he would stand out among his peers, who would all be wearing *tefillin*. As he approached the study hall, or just as he walked in, perhaps he was accosted by one of his colleagues, who may have had a look of shock or condemnation on his face. Everyone's eyes surely turned to him as he paced down the aisle, until one of the other students blurted out what had just happened, minutes beforehand. The aggrieved student must have realized that at least some of his peers believed the prostitute; after all, had the other students shouted her down and refused to accept her slander—had they waited to ask the student what happened, or presumed his innocence—he surely would not have felt such deep and intense shame. Instead, when he looked into the eyes of his friends, he must have seen at least some level of suspicion, some level of belief of the prostitute. He became scared, humiliated, ashamed, and angry—he recognized that based on the accusation of this prostitute, his stature, which he worked so hard to build, was diminished in the eyes of his friends and colleagues. It is in this context and in this moment, the student would do anything that he could to escape. Looking around and not seeing friends who would defend him and believe him, he tossed himself from the roof so that he would not have to bear the shame and humiliation brought on by this heinous accusation. In the words of Ms. Pierce, it is upsetting that he thought "this was his option."

Of course, this presentation takes certain interpretive liberties that are not explicit in the text of the Gemara; nevertheless, if this interpretation is accurate, it reflects a deeper reality noticed by contemporary researchers regarding the role of onlookers on the effect of bullying on the victim. Salmivalli[117] identifies four different roles that those present at the time of bullying can take: assistants of bullies, who join in with the bully in the behavior; reinforcers of bullies, who may cheer or laugh, even if they do not join; outsiders, who withdraw from the situation; and defenders of the victim, who actively take the side of the victim while offering defense, comfort, or support. Subsequently, Sainio[118] found that when victims had a defender, they had higher self-esteem and higher status among their peers, as well as being more likely to be victimized less. However, a full quarter of the victims in their study were without a defender, which was associated with being victimized more frequently, being

117. Salmivalli, C., Lagerspetz, K., Björkqvist, K., Österman, K., & Kaukiainen, A. (1996). Bullying as a group process: Participant roles and their relations to social status within the group. *Aggressive Behavior, 22,* 1–15.

118. Sainio, M., Veenstra, R., Huitsing, G., & Salmivalli, C. (2011). Victims and their defenders: A dyadic approach. *International Journal of Behavioral Development, 35*(2), 144-151.

more rejected and less well-liked by their peers. Similarly, one study found that a bystander's action on behalf of the victim was effective at stopping a bullying episode.[119]

Returning to story in the Gemara, the through their inaction, they enabled and emboldened the bully, which led to disastrous consequences. It is possible that in our case, the students, perhaps unwittingly, also played the role of a reinforcer for the bully. By not actively rejecting her claim, but instead perhaps believing it, they reinforced her awful behavior.

It is useful to consider what being a defender might look like in each of the scenarios described above. In the case of Jamel, perhaps it would mean teachers or administrators introducing an anti-bullying campaign in the school, and enforcing strict policies against bullying of other kids. Or, a defender could have come from other students, who would speak up vocally against those bullying and harassing Jamel; this defender might have befriended Jamel, and treated him with respect and dignity. In the case of the yeshiva student, the onlookers might have vocally stood up for their colleague and insisted that the students of the academy reserve any judgment until they spoke with the accused; they would have had a compassionate stance toward their friend as he walked in, instead of expressions of judgment and condemnation. As contemporary research has found, one way to avoid such terrible outcomes is to be a defender, and train our children and communities to be defenders. Unfortunately, too often, this is a lesson that we learn only in retrospect.

---

119. Lynn Hawkins, D., Pepler, D. J., & Craig, W. M. (2001). Naturalistic observations of peer interventions in bullying. *Social Development, 10*(4), 512-527.

The Story of Sarah and Hagar

The story cited in the Talmud, with its awful outcome, could be viewed as an isolated incident that requires minimal attention. However, the potential for catastrophic results from treating others with excessive harshness, and lessons about defending the victim, play a much more prominent role in Jewish thought, as described by the Rishonim, even affecting the entire course of human history. After many years of not bearing children, Sarah offered Avraham to marry Hagar as well, in order to have offspring from her; in accordance with Sarah's request, Avraham agreed to marry Hagar, and she subsequently became pregnant with a child. Hagar's success in conceiving a child led to her holding Sarah in lower esteem, which angered Sarah, who complained to Avraham:

> The outrage against me is due to you! It was I who gave my maidservant into your bosom, and when she saw that she had conceived, I became lowered in her esteem. Let Hashem judge between me and you!

The commentators broadly agree that Hagar acted inappropriately, and that that Sarah's complaint to Avraham was entirely justified. However, the proper understanding of the following verse is a significant debate among the Rishonim:

> Avram said to Sarai, "Behold, your maidservant is in your hand; do to her as you see fit." And Sarai dealt harshly with her, so [Hagar] fled from her (Bereishis 16:5-6).

Chazal are in general consensus that Sarah was correct to assert her authority in the home, even if that meant Hagar would be forced to leave. Nevertheless, several Rishonim see a grave mistake by both Sarah and Avraham in this verse,[120] as stated by Ramban:

> Our foremother sinned by perpetrating this oppression, as did Avraham by allowing it to happen. Hashem attended to her suffering and gave her a son who would be a *"perah adam"* who would oppress the descendants of Avraham and Sarah with all sorts of oppression.[121]

In this commentary, Ramban identifies the unnecessarily harsh treatment of Hagar at the hands of Sarah, as well as Avraham's failure to stick up for Hagar in the face of unkind treatment. However difficult of a reality this description presents, Ramban suggests an additional layer of impact of Sarah's and Avraham's actions—not only did it negatively affect Hagar, the residual effects continued for much longer. Yishmael is described as a *perah adam*, a challenging phrase to interpret, and commonly translated as a "wild-ass of a man." Remarkably, Ramban connects Sarah's treatment of Hagar with this description of Yishmael and his descendants. As Ramban explains (on *Bereishis* 16:12)

---

120. Many Rishonim and Acharonim disagree vehemently with Ramban and Radak, and argue that it is unconscionable to think that Avraham and Sarah would act in such a cruel way. My goal is not to weigh the merits of each side; rather, I intend to show that the insights emerging from Ramban's commentary are consistent with contemporary understanding of the impact of bullying.

121. Ramban seems to be echoing the commentary of Radak, who provides a more elaborate description of Sarah's and Avraham's wrongdoing.

this phrase, *perah adam*, refers to a pattern of aggression, that his descendants will "be at war with all of the other nations." Combining this with the previous passage in his commentary, it seems that this aggressive streak in Yishmael's descendants is a direct result of the treatment experienced by his mother.

Compare this account with the following paragraph, discussing those who are victims-turned-bullies:

> It should be noted that so-called bully-victims, who are themselves victimized and bully others, seem to be a distinct group from non-victimized bullies in many ways, also with respect to the reasons for their attacks. Rather than skillful and strategic children, bully-victims seem to be dysregulated, hot-tempered, and high on both proactive and reactive aggression.[122]

Those who are victimized and become bullies themselves exhibit a tendency toward aggressive behavior that is of a different type than other type of bullying. Instead of being strategic, with a certain goal in mind, which researchers assume is related to gaining some type of elevated status, these types of bullies are driven by states of dysregulation and temper—in other words, *perah adam*.

According to Ramban, the millennia-long battle between descendants of Yitzchak and those of Yishmael can be traced back to the reaction Hagar and Yishmael had to Sarah's and Avraham's treatment. As Rabbi Dovid Kimchi (Radak) writes, this episode is recorded in the Torah "so that a person can [study it and] acquire

---

122. Salmivalli, 2010.

good character traits, and distance himself from bad character traits." Just as the impact that this victim-bully transition has had on Jewish and human history is immeasurable, so too bullying can have an immeasurably negative effect on victims of bullying in school, the workplace, and in society at large. It is our responsibility to do our part to create an environment that does not allow for bullying to take place, and to defend the victims in the unfortunate event that bullying does happen.

To Be or Not To Be a Defender

As described above, both Chazal and contemporary psychological literature identify the importance of the response of onlookers in response to bullying. However, a major difference between their perspectives is that the psychological literature focuses on the benefits of defending the victim, whereas Chazal mostly focus on the obligation of bystanders, summarized by the Rabbinic dictum: "because they could have effectively protested, but they did not protest" (e.g., *Shabbos* 54b). Despite this general rule, that a person is required to protest and defend a victim of bullying, Chazal also accept that there are times that a bystander may not be able to effectively act in support of the victim, and taking on the role of "outsider" or "reinforcer" may be preferable to being a "defender."

The Hebrew word most akin to being a "reinforcer" is *chanifah*, which is often translated as "flattery." In this context, *chanifah* refers to a person siding with the bully, even providing affirming statements, in order to gain favor in the eyes of the bully. Generally speaking, Chazal have a very negative attitude towards those who reinforce the actions of bullies (e.g., *Sotah* 41b), except in circumstances that failing to be a reinforcer would put the individual in harm's way (see the story of Ullah, *Nedarim* 22a; story of Rabbi Dostai bar Rabbi Yannai, *Gittin* 14b).

When being a defender is not possible, taking the stance of an outsider is clearly much preferred to being a reinforcer, as highlighted in the Gemara's story involving King Agrippas, part of the Herodian dynasty who ruled shortly before the destruction of the Second Temple (*Sotah* 41a-b). Agrippas's lineage disqualified him from being the king, despite which he seized power. Although Agrippas was not a bully in the classic sense, it is instructive to consider how Chazal viewed those who responded to his inappropriate takeover of the monarchy. The Mishnah there describes the king's role during the *Hak'hel* service, during which the king is meant to read from the book of *Devarim*. In the course of telling the story, the Mishnah records a story involving Agrippas:

> King Agrippas arose, and received the Torah scroll, and read from it while standing… when Agrippas arrived at the verse in the portion read by the king that states: "You may not appoint a foreigner over you" tears flowed from his eyes [because although his mother was Jewish, his father was not]. The nation said to him: Fear not, Agrippas. You are our brother, you are our brother.

Although the Mishnah seems to regard Agrippas positively for taking to heart the mitzvah that would preclude his ability to be king, the Gemara condemns the Jewish people for their response:

138

It is taught in the name of Rabbi Natan: At that moment the Jewish people were sentenced to destruction for flattering Agrippas.

Tosafos wonders what was so terrible about the response of the Jewish people—why did their supportive words towards Agrippas merit such a harsh punishment? His answer is that

...this was the flattery, that Agrippas ascended to the kingship by force against the laws of the Torah, and the people acquiesced to him and strengthened his position through their supportive words. Granted they were not in the position to protest [as they would be putting themselves in danger], but they should have remained quiet and not strengthened Agrippas.

In other words, Agrippas coerced his way into becoming the ruler. Tosafos recognizes that the Jewish people could not have taken the role of "defender," given the power and authority that Agrippas wielded. Nevertheless, Tosafos argues that the Gemara condemns the Jewish people for taking the role of "reinforcer," instead of recognizing that they could have taken a stance of "outsider" toward Agrippas' actions.

What emerges from this analysis is that of the four approaches a bystander can take in response to bullying, taking the stance of either defender or outsider may be the most advisable; however, it is not clear how a person is meant to decide which course of action is best in any particular situation. Indeed, this question of whether to be a defender or an outsider may be the central question in the crucial sequence of events leading to the destruction of the second *Beis Ha-Mikdash,* as the Gemara famously records in the story of Kamtza and Bar Kamtza (*Gittin* 55b-56a).

As the story goes, a wealthy Jew was throwing a party and asked his servant to invite a certain friend (Kamtza), but the servant accidentally invited a similarly named foe instead (Bar Kamtza). The party's host instructed Bar Kamtza to leave, and Bar Kamtza pleaded with the host to not embarrass him, and tried to negotiate a price for which the host would allow him to stay. The host refused, and out of anger toward the Rabbis who were present and said nothing, the exiled guest committed himself to antagonizing the Jewish community. Bar Kamtza devised a plan to aggravate the Rabbis: he reported to the Caesar that the Jews were rebelling, and suggested that the Caesar send an offering to test the Jew's loyalty to him. On the way to the Temple with Caesar's animal, Bar Kamtza made a small blemish that would be negligible to the Caesar, but would disqualify the animal from being offered on the *mizbeach* (altar). The Gemara records that the Rabbis had a discussion about what to do. First, they wanted to offer the animal, but Rabbi Zechariah ben Avkolas objected, saying that doing so would demonstrate to the general population that blemished animals may be brought on the *mizbeach.* The next option, they thought, was to kill Bar Kamtza, as he was threatening their lives by bringing false accusations about the Jewish community to the Caesar. Again Rabbi Zechariah ben Avkolas objected, saying that the general population would learn from this episode that someone who causes a blemish in an animal is liable for the death penalty. And so, as it was, the animal was rejected, word was reported back to the Caesar, and the destruction of the *Beis Ha-Mikdash* ensued. If this were the whole story, a powerful lesson could be learned regarding the catastrophic effect of bullying; just as Ramban above argues that the mistreatment of Yishmael led to many years of antagonism at his descendants' hands, so too, here, did the host's bullying of Bar Kamtza lead to terrible long-term destruction for the Jewish people.

The Gemara there, however, makes a remarkable statement attributing blame for the destruction of the Temple.

Rabbi Yochanan says: The humility of Rabbi Zechariah ben Avkolas destroyed our Temple, burned our Sanctuary, and exiled us from our land.

The commentators try to understand the basis for Rabbi Yochanan's attribution of blame upon Rabbi Zechariah. Rashi comments that Rabbi Zechariah should have permitted the killing of Bar Kamtza, so as not to allow him to return a negative report to the Caesar. Maharsha and others suggest that he should have permitted the sacrifice to be brought on the altar. Rabbi Zvi Hirsch Chajes (Maharatz Chajes) understand that this "humility" refers to a discomfort considering himself fit to make this type of decision in the first place.

However, an alternate version of the story found in the Midrash (*Eichah Rabbah* 4:2) suggests a different explanation.[123] In the Midrash, instead of reporting generically that the Rabbis were present, a specific rabbi, Rabbi Zechariah ben Avkolas, was identified as the rabbi who was in the position to defend Bar Kamtza against

---

123. E.g., Maharam Shif.

141

the host's pressure. According to this view, Rabbi Zechariah should have identified that Bar Kamtza was being unfairly humiliated, and should have taken a stand as a defender for Bar Kamtza. Had Rabbi Zechariah done so, the Midrash implies that this defense by a Rabbinic representative would have been sufficient for Bar Kamtza not to seek revenge, which would have served to obviate the sequence of catastrophic events that followed. Instead, Rabbi Zechariah adopted the role of an outsider; he refused to take sides in defense of the victim, Bar Kamtza, which set into motion the events that would lead to the destruction of the *Beis Ha-Mikdash*.[124]

---

124. This alleged error by Rabbi Zechariah ben Avkolas does not appear to be a temporary lack of clarity; this approach of not taking sides and avoiding controversy seems to be a general principle that he followed, based on the following Tosefta, *Shabbos* 17:4. The Tosefta records a disagreement between Beis Hillel and Beis Shammai regarding the laws of muktzeh and what a person should do with the bones and seed-shells after one eats. Beis Hillel rules that one may remove them, whereas Beis Shammai rules that one should lift the table and shake off the bones or shells. The Tosefta then cites Rabbi Zechariah ben Avkolas who "does not rule like Beis Shammai or Beis Hillel; instead he tosses [the bones or shells] under his chair [as he eats, so as to not have to move the bones or shells after he eats]." The *halachah* ends with a comment that seems to be entirely unrelated: "Rabbi Yose says: the humility of Rabbi Zechariah ben Avkolas burned the Sanctuary." What Rabbi Yose seems to be adding is that Rabbi Zechariah's general approach to avoid taking sides in a debate is the cause of his practice regarding *muktzeh*, as well as his practice in the story of Bar Kamtza. Rabbi Yose seems to be condemning this approach, preferring Rabbi Zechariah to take the side he thinks is correct.

Lesson for Today

Both Chazal and contemporary researchers have identified the potentially catastrophic outcomes associated with bullying, as well as the crucial role that onlookers can play in mitigating the harm. Of course, there is no definitive rule for how spectators should react to a bullying situation, as each situation has its own features and risks. Nevertheless, it is clear from Chazal, and from modern research, that the common response of ignoring the situation is both psychologically harmful and morally deficient. Perhaps the most succinct example of Chazal's charge to take a stand is found in a Gemara describing Pharaoh's consultation regarding how to deal with the Jewish people:

> Rabbi Chiya bar Abba says that Rabbi Simai says: Three people were consulted [by Pharaoh] in that counsel: Bil'am, Iyov, and Yisro. Bil'am, who advised Pharaoh to kill all sons born to the Jewish people, was punished by being killed in the war with Midian. Iyov, who was silent and neither advised nor protested, was punished by suffering.... Yisro, who ran away [as a sign of protest], merited that some of his children's children sat in the Sanhedrin in the Chamber of Hewn Stone (*Sotah* 11a).

In my clinical experience, most people choose to not get involved in these types of circumstances, as it is emotionally uncomfortable, and standing up for a victim carries its own risk; people often rationalize the decision not to get involved by saying that their defense of a victim would not make a difference or it is not their place. While this rationalization may sometimes be justified, when we combine the insights from modern research with the tremendous benefit that defending victims can have, as well as the moral imperative highlighted by Chazal to do all that we can to defend the vulnerable, we can see the importance of training both ourselves and our youth to be sensitive to the presence of bullying, and gain the skills to become effective defenders. By becoming people willing to take a stand in favor of the marginalized, we are fulfilling Chazal's spiritual and moral guidance, as well as creating a supportive environment for those who are struggling.

Is That Your Final Answer?
Toch Kedei Dibbur,
Cross-cultural Studies, and Neuroscience (27b)

וְאִם נָתַן לוֹ וְלֹא הֶחֱזִיר — נִקְרָא "גַּזְלָן" ,
שֶׁנֶּאֱמַר: "וְאַתֶּם בְּעַרְתֶּם הַכֶּרֶם גְּזֵלַת הֶעָנִי בְּבָתֵּיכֶם".

If the other person extended his greeting to him and he did not respond,
he is called a robber, as it is stated: "It is you who have eaten up the
vineyard, the spoils of the poor is in your houses" (Yeshayahu 3:14)
— Berachos 6b

Brian Regan, a famously clean comedian, describes his exasperation at a friend teaching him to play chess.[125] When his friend makes a move, he holds his finger on top of the piece and says, "It's not an official move until I take my finger off." Regan wonders, "Wouldn't it be great if you could do that in life? If you're going to do something, and you're not quite sure whether it's the right move, just protect yourself." The bit peaks as he imagines a bank robber storming a bank screaming, "I WANT EVERYBODY'S MONEY!" But with a finger on his head, looks cautiously around and says, "Okay, I'm not gonna do this...."

---

125. *All by Myself,* Brian Regan, 2011.

Indeed, in *halachah*, there is such a mechanism, known as *toch kedei dibbur (ke-dibbur damei)*—literally "within the time for speech (is considered one speech)"—and this principle is applied in virtually all areas of *halachah*, aside from several limited situations specified by the Gemara (*Nedarim* 87). *Toch kedei dibbur* operates differently in different circumstances, sometimes functioning as a "do-over" period, sometimes connecting two statements,[126] and sometimes simply representing a short period of time. Rishonim and Acharonim offer a variety of explanations regarding its source (Torah vs. Rabbinic), whether an action is considered completed prior to the end of this period, and the exact measurement of the period of time (greeting one's teacher as opposed to greeting one's student). Although contemporary psychological science is certainly not interested in the application of *toch kedei dibbur*, two areas of study—one in cross-cultural research, and the other in neuropsychology—may have bearing on this *halachah*.

Culture and Toch Kedei Dibbur[127]

According to Rabbeinu Tam,[128] *toch kedei dibbur* is a Rabbinic institution based on a somewhat unexpected calculation. The Gemara in *Berachos* (6b) likens someone who does not return a greeting to someone who steals from the poor, and, as such, the expectation is that

---

126. E.g., if someone accepts *nezirus*, and another person says, "and me too," if the second statement comes within *toch kedei dibbur*, the second person is a *nazir*; otherwise, he is not.

127. The following discussion may not be consistent with every explanation of *toch kedei dibbur*; for that reason, in this section, I am dealing specifically within the view of Rabbeinu Tam.

128. Tosafos, *Bava Kamma* 73b, s.v. *ki leis lei le-Rabbi Yosi*.

a person is meant to reciprocate the greeting. Accordingly, Rabbeinu Tam argues that if Chazal require one to respond, they must also allow for the length of that response not to interfere with either rituals or monetary transactions. In other words, Rabbeinu Tam's opinion is that because Chazal expect a person to act respectfully towards others and offer or return a proper greeting, they must make an allowance for this amount of time to be considered negligible, and the actions taken within this time to be contiguous.

Based on this understanding, we might assume that the duration of *toch kedei dibbur* is the amount of time necessary for a standard greeting from one person to another, as one opinion states in the Talmud Yerushalmi, "the amount of time for one person to greet his friend" (*Berachos* 2:1). However, the Talmud Bavli does not record this view, and instead presents two alternate opinions: the amount of time for a teacher to greet his student (*"shalom aleichem"*), or the longer greeting required of a student greeting his teacher (*"shalom aleichem rebbi [u-mori]"*). How are we meant to understand this disagreement?

Perhaps one answer to this question is related to an area studied by cross-cultural researchers, namely how respect is communicated among different groups of people.[129] On a practical level, this line of inquiry is most relevant to military personnel,[130] international

---

129. Mackenzie, L., & Wallace, M. (2011). The communication of respect as a significant dimension of cross-cultural communication competence. *Cross-Cultural Communication, 7*(3), 10-18.

130. E.g., Hancock, P. A., Szalma, J. L., & van Driel, M. (2007). An initial framework for enhancing cultural competency: The science of cultural readiness (No. DEOMI-CCC-07-2). Defense equal opportunity management(retrieved from https://apps.dtic.mil/sti/pdfs/ADA488614.pdf).

business dealings,[131] or education. Consider the following vignette and excerpt related to cultural differences between a principle in New Zealand of European origin, and a recent Samoan immigrant to New Zealand:[132]

> Tino, a young Samoan boy who had recently arrived in New Zealand, was summoned to the office of the school principal for being repeatedly late for school. He knocked on the door of the principal's office. When he was told to come in, he walked in with hunched shoulders, scuttled over to a chair and sat down without being asked to do so by the principal. In response to the principal's questions, he either said nothing or he muttered, "I don't know." He looked down at the floor throughout the interview and never met the principal's eyes.
>
> From the principal's perspective... Tino's hunched posture seemed an uncooperative stance, possibly expressing resentment, and Tino should have waited until asked to sit down in the office of a superior. Tino's avoidance of the principal's eyes was also interpreted as evasive behavior.
>
> In fact, Tino's communicative behavior followed culturally appropriate norms for expressing respect to a

131. E.g., Carté, P., & Fox, C. (2008). *Bridging the culture gap: A practical guide to international business communication.* Kogan Page Publishers.

132. Holmes, J. (2012). Politeness in Intercultural Discourse and Communication. In C. B. Paulston, S. F. Kiesling and E. S. Rangel (Eds), *The handbook of intercultural discourse and communication.* Chichester, UK: John Wiley & Sons.

superior in Samoan culture. A bowed posture is respectful, since one must attempt to keep oneself at a lower level than the superior; for the same reason, Tino sat down as quickly as possible. Keeping one's eyes lowered is similarly a signal of respect; and it is not appropriate in Samoan culture for Tino to "answer back." Subordinates are expected to listen to reprimands in silence.

Although this vignette represents a single anecdote, an important general lesson emerges from the interaction between the student and his school principal. The principal possessed a set of assumptions about what appropriate, respectful behavior looks like among students in his school, which were consistent with his own background and training. At the same time, the new immigrant had a similar value for demonstrating respect, except his method for showing respect differed dramatically from the methods present in his new home culture. Indeed, the same act that can be seen as standard expressions of respect and deference by one person may be viewed as disrespectful and irreverent by someone from a different culture.

A similar type of disagreement seems to be the center of a disagreement and story described in the Talmud and Rishonim. The Gemara (*Berachos* 27b), while presenting a number of *halachos* related to how one should show respect for one's teacher, rules that a person "should not greet one's teacher." The Rishonim argue regarding the intent of this statement. It might mean that a person should not greet his teacher as he would a regular person—"*shalom alecha*"—and instead should add an additional word to the phrase "*shalom alecha rebbi*."[133] A second opinion is that it means a person should not greet one's teacher at all.[134] According to the latter view, that a student should not greet a teacher, how are we meant to understand the position of one side in the Gemara[135] that *toch kedei dibbur* is the length of the greeting from a student to a teacher? Rabbeinu Yonah (on *Berachos* 27b) explains that this position refers to the requirement of a student to *respond* to his teacher if the teacher extends a greeting, but the student should not *initiate* a greeting of his own volition.

This debate regarding whether one may either initiate or respond to a greeting from his teacher has bearing on the *halachah* of *toch kedei dibbur*. As noted by a number of Rishonim, the way a student might *greet* his teacher would be "*shalom alecha rebbi*" (three words), while the way he would *respond* to a teacher greeting would be "*shalom alecha rebbi u-mori*" (four words).[136] Similarly, the Rishonim and Acharonim disagree regarding the correct text of the Gemara in *Bava Kamma* which describes the duration of *toch kedei dibbur*, as the standard texts reads "*shalom alecha rebbi u-mori*," indicating that one may only respond to a teacher greeting; other Rishonim[137] have an alternate text with only three words, "*shalom alecha rebbi*,"

133. E.g., Rashi, ad loc.; Tosafos, *Bava Kamma* 73b, s.v. *kedei she'elas talmid la-rav*.
134. Rabbeinu Yonah, ad loc.
135. *Bava Kamma* 73b; *Nazir* 20b; TY *Berachos* 2:1 (13a).
136. Rambam, *Hilchos Talmud Torah* 5:5. This seems to be in contrast to the Talmud Yerushalmi in *Berachos* 2:1, in which Rabbi Yochanan is quoted as saying that the greeting of a teacher to a student is "*shalom alecha rebbi*."
137. See Ritva, *Nedarim* 86b, Mossad Ha-Rav Kook edition note 238 for various sources.

suggesting that one may initiate a greeting to his teacher.

Based on the Gemaras presented above, one could argue that that disagreement about the length of *toch kedei dibbur* is not an issue of *culture*, but rather differences of opinion regarding optimal ways to show respect developed through examination of earlier Rabbinic sources. However, a story recorded in the Talmud Yerushalmi (*Berachos* 13a) provides strong evidence that one's cultural background imparts norms for how to show respect to others:

> Rabbi Yochanan was [walking and] leaning on Rabbi Yaakov bar Idi, and Rabbi Elazar saw him [from a distance] and hid from him. Rabbi Yochanan said [to Rabbi Yaakov bar Idi]: "This Babylonian [Rabbi Elazar] commits two offenses against me. The first is that he does not greet me." ... [Rabbi Yaakov bar Idi] responded: "This is how they conduct themselves in [Babylonia], a young scholar does not greet his superior, as they fulfill the verse, 'Youths would see me and conceal themselves' (Iyov 29:8)." ... [Rabbi Yochanan] replied: "Rabbi Yaakov bar Idi, you know how to pacify me!"

As we see from this passage, Rabbi Yochanan, who was the leading scholar in Israel at the time, was upset that his student, Rabbi Elazar, avoided the opportunity to greet him, which he considered disrespectful. As the Gemara elaborates, Rabbi Elazar, who came from Babylonia, seemed to be faced with a dilemma. On the one hand, he understood that not greeting Rabbi Yochanan would be considered disrespectful; on the other hand, based on his own training and sensitivities, he was accustomed to the practice that one does not greet a superior—even to respond to a greeting—and he would have been uncomfortable offering a greeting to Rabbi Yochanan in violation of that sensitivity. As a result, he decided the best course of action was to avoid the situation altogether. Of course, it stands to reason that Rabbi Elazar's practice, which the Gemara suggests is in fulfillment of a textually-based value, was not due to blind acceptance of cultural practice, but instead was the result of a deliberate conclusion that this approach best fulfilled the requirements of respect towards one's teacher; similarly, Rabbi Yochanan's practice also resulted from a measured assessment of the proper way to demonstrate respect. Nevertheless, the story appears to indicate that Rabbi Elazar's native cultural milieu helped furnish him with the way the sensitivity towards respect was manifest, which was at odds with the cultural norm familiar to Rabbi Yochanan. Based on this reading, within the opinion of Rabbeinu Tam, the disagreement regarding the length of *toch kedei dibbur*, at least in part, is an expression of cross-cultural differences in displays of respect.

A separate passage in the Talmud (*Shabbos* 89a) supports this idea that displays of respect through greetings is a function of cultural norms and differences:

And Rabbi Yehoshua ben Levi said: When Moshe ascended on High [to receive the Torah], he found the Holy One, Blessed be He, tying crowns to letters. [Moshe said nothing and Hashem] said to him: *"Moshe, is there no greeting in your city?"* Moshe said before Him: "Does a servant greet his master?" (i.e., that would be disrespectful). [Hashem] said to him, "At least you should have supported Me." Immediately Moshe said to Hashem: "And now, may the power of the Lord be magnified as you have spoken" (*Bamidbar* 14:17).

When Moshe ascended to receive the Torah, he entered the domain of Hashem and the ministering angels.[138] Like Rabbi Elazar in Israel, Moshe was a cultural outsider, the only human being to ascend to be with angels. Hashem, being sensitive to Moshe's unfamiliarity with the norms of the Heavens asks him, "Moshe, is there no greeting in your city?" instead of a more direct, and perhaps more harsh option, such as "Moshe, you should have greeted Me!" As the question suggests, how, whether, and to whom we extend greetings was regarded, at least to some extent, as a function of cultural norms.

Lesson for Today, Part 1

For any mental health professional, "cultural competence" is a central feature of her or his training. There is an understanding that although there are certainly large differences between individuals of any individual culture, a person's culture has an impact over how he sees the world, and, as such, may impact how a mental health professional can best interact with him. As we find in the passages from the Gemara, what is seen as the height of respect by one person from one culture may be seen as an act of grave disrespect

---

138. As another passage in *Shabbos* 89a writes: "And Rabbi Yehoshua ben Levi said: When Moshe ascended on High to receive the Torah, the ministering angels said before the Holy One, Blessed be He: Master of the Universe, what is one born of a woman doing here among us?"

by a person from another culture. Indeed, this lesson is relevant for mental health professionals and lay-people alike.

Despite the importance of cross-cultural understanding, for me, the most significant message of Rabbeinu Tam's understanding is the supreme importance placed on showing respect. For Rabbeinu Tam, addressing others respectfully, including to those who are impoverished and disenfranchised, is so important that Chazal introduced the concept *toch kedei dibbur* in order to allow the treatment of others with basic dignity not to interfere negatively with ritual practice or monetary transactions. Increasingly, particularly with the popularity of smartphones and similar devices, we keep to ourselves and may not engage with strangers in our neighborhood. However, the lesson of *toch kedei dibbur* is that the basic demonstration recognizing the dignity of another person should be central to our lives.

Neuroscience and Toch Kedei Dibbur

Most Rishonim disagree with Rabbeinu Tam's position that *toch kedei dibbur* is of Rabbinic origin based on the need to greet others. Rabbi Nissim ben Reuven of Girona (Ran) (*Nedarim* 87a) directly rejects Rabbeinu Tam's interpretation and asserts that *toch kedei dibbur* is a Torah-based principle rooted in the idea that people do not act with complete intent in most circumstances, and, as such, they are given the latitude to reverse a statement or decision within a few seconds of making it—like the finger on the chess piece.

An obvious question regarding Ran's position is: What is so magical about this amount of time? According to Rabbeinu Tam, Chazal specified this amount of time to ensure that a person could fulfill his obligation to greet others and not lose out on a business transaction or ritual requirement. However, according Ran, there does not appear to be a clear reason why this length of time, roughly 2-3 seconds, is the amount of time permitted to finalize one's thoughts. Contemporary neuroscience may shed some light on the significance of this amount of time.

A major question considered by cognitive psychologists, dating back close to 150 years,[139] focuses on how people convert sensory information into short- or long-term memory. Most researchers agree that there exist brain functions that essentially hold sensory information—either visual or auditory—for a short period of time without encoding it into short- or long-term memory. The function responsible for auditory or verbal information is known as the "phonological loop," which includes one function that stores the information very briefly and is subject to rapid decay, and a second function that allows a person to rehearse this information internally to extend its presence in one's mind. One of the main researchers gives the following description:[140]

It is assumed to contain a temporary storage system in which acoustic or speech-based information can be held in the form of memory traces that spontaneously fade away within 2 or 3 seconds unless refreshed by rehearsal.

139. Eggert, G.H., ed. and trans. Early Sources in Aphasia and Related Disorders. Vol. I. *Wernicke's works on aphasia: A sourcebook and review.* The Hague, The Netherlands: Mouton Publishers, 1977.
140. Baddeley, A. (1996). The fractionation of working memory. *Proceedings of the National Academy of Sciences, 93*(24), 13468-13472.

One way to think about this phonological store is like an echo over a canyon where, for a few seconds, the sound can be heard reverberating. Similarly, when we hear information, the sound reverberates in our mind before being encoded. Within that time, we can access it, rehearse it, and potentially encode it; after that time, the traces of the sound are gone.

Although this phonological loop is something of a theoretical construct, other researchers have used brain-imaging technology to try to identify which structural parts of the brain may be responsible for such a system. A full discussion of the various areas of the brain, their general functions, and how their involvement in the phonological loop helps us understand the process, is well beyond the scope of this chapter. Nevertheless, studies using fMRI techniques have identified a few neural structures, mostly in the parietal lobe, that seem to be involved in the very-short-term echoic storage of auditory or verbal information.[141] When we speak, hear others speak, or even think quietly in our minds, the phonological stimuli remain active in our brains for a few seconds, even after the physical elements of sound have dissipated. Functionally, this ability allows a person to decide whether to focus on this information and rehearse or encode it, or to ignore it and allow the traces of the memory to disappear.

It is possible that this phenomenon may underlie the Ran's understanding of *toch kedei dibbur*. For a couple of seconds, the words that we say, or thoughts that we think, are not yet over, so they are not yet final. After this time, the verbal or auditory information

---

141. Buchsbaum, B. R., & D'Esposito, M. (2008). The search for the phonological store: From loop to convolution. *Journal of Cognitive Neuroscience, 20*(5), 762-778.

is considered final as the final echoes of the sound have not only disappeared from the environment, but they have also disappeared from our brain, barring retention due to rehearsal. Indeed, this idea can be found in the commentary of Rabbi Yom Tov Asevilli (Ritva) (*Nedarim* 89b), who explains that "the Chachamim stated that for this length of time one's lips are still articulating the first statement, and it is as though he is still speaking."[142]

This approach, that assumes auditory or verbal information remains extant in our brains even after the physical sound is gone, can help explain a different passage in the Talmud that, on its surface, seems odd. The Gemara (*Megillah* 27b) records the *halachah* that while praying, one must wait the amount of time required to walk four cubits (roughly 2-3 seconds) before urinating. Rav Ashi offers an explanation for this ruling:

> Rav Ashi said: Because for all the time it takes to walk four cubits, his prayer is still arranged in his mouth, and his lips are still articulating them.

Surely, Chazal did not think that for several seconds after uttering a prayer one's lips are still vibrating! According to the approach above, however, this rule is very understandable. Even after a person completes his prayer, his mind retains the words and sound of prayer for a couple of seconds—for this person, his prayer has not yet ended. As such it would be inappropriate to relieve oneself while his mind is still engaged in prayer.

---

142. In a personal note from Rabbi Mendel Blachman, he stated that Ritva is in agreement with Ran that *toch kedei dibbur* is a Torah rule, not of rabbinic origin.

It is also possible that this approach can help explain perhaps the most perplexing application of *toch kedei dibbur* found in the Talmud regarding rending one's garment upon hearing about the death of a close relative. The Gemara (*Nedarim* 87a) cites two opposing *baraisos*: one rules that someone who rent his garment upon misinformation that a certain relative died, and then receives the correct report that a different relative actually passed away, did not fulfill his obligation to rend his garment and must rend it again; the second *baraisa* seems to rule in a similar case that one does fulfill his obligation and need not rend again. Rav Ashi resolves this contradiction using the rules of *toch kedei dibbur*: if one was correctly informed within the period of *toch kedei dibbur*, then he fulfilled his obligation to rend his garment; if he was corrected following *toch kedei dibbur*, he must re-tear his garment.

Tosafos comments that in the instance Chazal ruled that the individual has fulfilled his obligation for *kri'ah* (rending garments), it is considered as if he rent his garment after hearing the correction. How are we to understand that a person can fulfill his obligation for *kri'ah* before hearing that a relative passed away? According to Rashbam, it is possible that two events that happen within *toch kedei dibbur* of each other are considered simultaneous (*Bava Basra* 129b). According to Tosafos, it could simply be a leniency regarding *kri'ah* (*Bava Kamma* 73b). However, according what we stated above, we may offer an additional approach. Apparently, as is evident from the context of this Gemara, tearing one's garment is considered a type of speech, or at least equivalent to speech in some qualities. As such, when one rips his clothes, the anguish expressed by rending the garments, which may be considered an integral element of the tearing ritual, is not completed when one finishes the act of tearing. Instead, it lingers for a couple seconds, as the thoughts and words associated with the anguish would be retained for a brief period in this phonological store; this retention of the verbal aspects of the anguish extends the act of tearing until the thoughts associated with it dissipate, which, in the case of the Gemara that does not require re-tearing his garment, turned out to be after the person received the new corrected information about his deceased relative.

Lesson for Today, Part 2

Nuances of neuroscience typically do not provide obvious lessons about life, and it is impossible to determine whether the insight described above is actually related to the principle of *toch kedei dibbur*. Nevertheless, pondering the intricate, though still largely unknown, processes of human brain functioning, and how what we learn relates to our understanding of Hashem and His Torah, fulfills the following instruction of Rambam (*Hilchos Yesodei ha-Torah* 2:2-3):

> What is the path [to attain] love and fear of Him? When a person contemplates His wondrous and great deeds and creations and appreciates His infinite wisdom that surpasses all comparison, he will immediately love, praise, and glorify [Him], yearning with tremendous desire to know [God's] great name, as David stated: "My soul thirsts for the Lord, for the living God" (*Tehillim* 42:3). When he [continues] to reflect on these same matters, he will immediately recoil in awe and fear, appreciating how he is a tiny, lowly, and dark creature, standing with his flimsy, limited, wisdom before

He who is of perfect knowledge, as David stated: "When I see Your heavens, the work of Your fingers... [I wonder] what is man that You should recall Him" (*Tehillim* 8:4-5).

Studying how the brain works may be of particular significance, as it is the vehicle driving our thoughts, knowledge, and, ultimately, our behavior; as Rav Chaim of Volozhen wrote (*Nefesh ha-Chaim* 1:14-15, based on the *Zohar*), to whatever extent a person's *neshamah* (soul) is housed in his body, its location is the brain. As the brain is such a central organ to both physical and spiritual life, it should not be surprising that there may exist overlap between features of brain functioning and aspects of Torah or *halachah*. The more we learn about how the brain operates, the deeper our appreciation of God's wonderous creation can be.

The IKEA effect (31b)

אָמְרָה לֵיהּ "אֶל הַנַּעַר הַזֶּה הִתְפַּלָּלְתִּי"

It is this child for whom I prayed

— Shmuel I 1:27

As the story goes, in the 1950's, General Mills hired a psychologist by the name of Ernest Dichter to help increase sales for its Betty Crocker brand of cakes mixes. After running a series of focus groups with various recipes, Dichter determined that instant cake mixes, which included powdered eggs and required virtually no effort to make, were less desirable to homemakers; he argued that, from a psychological perspective, the instant cake mixes undervalued the baker's labor and skill. Instead, he suggested, Betty Crocker's mixes should require the baker to put in a fresh egg, thereby giving the impression that the cake maker was putting in more effort and skill into the baking process; according to reports, Betty Crocker sales spiked following this change.[143]

This story, though perhaps somewhat exaggerated, presents a confusing result: adding one's own labor, which, in theory, should decrease the perceived value of the item, actually raised the value.[144]

143. Shapiro, L. (2004). *Something from the oven: Reinventing dinner in 1950s America*. New York: Viking

144. Notably, researchers debate the psychological mechanism at play to help explain this effect, with cognitive dissonance and

Only in recent years have social scientists given a name to this phenomenon—the "IKEA effect"[145]—which is similar to a long-recognized effect known as "effort justification." The popularity of this effect probably has to do with its catchy name, which is more memorable than a name used by other scientists in an earlier study, the "I designed it myself" effect.[146] The IKEA effect refers to the counterintuitive increase in a self-made product's valuation as compared to products that are made by others, and so named because people are willing to pay high prices for items from IKEA, even though consumers must put the item together themselves.

The 2012 paper naming this principle has been cited, at the time of this writing, over 600 times by subsequent studies, indicating the new interest this paper spawned. However, a careful read of several passages suggests that this principle, that something is more valuable when one's own effort has helped the create the product, was well-known to Chazal and used in both aggadic (non-legal, often metaphoric or moral teachings) and halachic contexts.

Examples of the IKEA Effect in Chazal

As we learn in Sefer Shmuel, Chana was unable to bear children for years. During one of the family pilgrimages to Shiloh, Chana's

---

relative contrast being two leading theories. See, for example, Zentall, T. R. (2010). Justification of effort by humans and pigeons: cognitive dissonance or contrast?. *Current Directions in Psychological Science, 19*(5), 296-300.

145. Norton, M. I., Mochon, D., & Ariely, D. (2012). The IKEA effect: When labor leads to love. *Journal of Consumer Psychology, 22*(3), 453-460.

146. Franke, N., Schreier, M., & Kaiser, U. (2010). The "I designed it myself" effect in mass customization. *Management Science, 56*(1), 125-140.

husbands second wife, Penina, disparaged Chana, as Penina had borne children, and Chana had not. In a moment of particular distress, Chana recited a tear-filled, sincere prayer, and offered the following vow: "Hashem, Master of Legions, if You take note of the suffering of Your maidservant...and give Your maidservant male offspring, then I shall give him to Hashem all the days of his life..." (1 Shmuel 1:11). And so it was that Chana was blessed with a son, whom she named Shmuel, and when he was a young child she fulfilled her part of the bargain and brought him back to Shiloh to serve Eli, the high priest, in God's house in Shiloh.

The Gemara in *Berachos* (31b) cites a series of Midrashim related to the conversations between Chana and Eli when she returned with Shmuel to deliver him to serve in the Temple. One Midrash tells a story in which Shmuel was nearly put to death for offering a halachic ruling in the presence of Eli, his teacher. According Rabbi Elazar, Shmuel ruled, correctly, that a priest need not slaughter a *korban*, and only at the next stage of the offering, receiving the blood in a bowl, is the mitzvah incumbent on the priest alone. Eli rebuked Shmuel, citing the *halachah* that one who rules in the presence of his teacher is subject to death. Upon hearing this Chana came to protest Shmuel's punishment, pleading that Eli not punish the child that she had prayed for. Eli replied: "Let me punish him, and I will pray for mercy, that the Holy One, Blessed be He, will grant you a son [who will be greater than this one]." She said to him: "For this youth I prayed [and I want no other]."

A number of explanations seem to be possible for Chana's reply. One could have understood that she was simply begging for mercy, as she had prayed for so long and suffered so greatly to have a child. Alternatively, perhaps she was highlighting the unfairness of the irony to Eli, that it would have been specifically her deal with God during her prayers to bring her son to serve in the Temple that would have led to his demise. Maharsha explains Chana's successful argument back to Eli in a different manner:

> [In other words, Chana was saying that] this child who was born to me through my own prayers is more dear to me than a different child who is born to me through your prayers.

Maharsha seems to be using the principle of the IKEA effect to explain why Chana is unwilling to accept this offer made by Eli. Despite being promised a son even greater than Shmuel, and despite apparently accepting the validity of the punishment that Eli wanted to mete out to Shmuel, she rejects that offer because her own efforts, through her own prayer, made Shmuel so much more valuable to her than any other child could be. Perhaps most remarkably, Eli accepts this argument and does not put Shmuel to death, indicating that this reason was sufficient for Chana not to accept his deal and to continue to beg for his mercy.

A second example of effort justification is found in the Midrash (*Bereishis Rabbah* 59:8), in the story of Avraham sending Eliezer to find a wife for his son, Yitzchak. Avraham wants to ensure that Eliezer does not select a wife from the local Canaanite population, so he has Eliezer swear that he will go to Avraham's birthplace to retrieve a wife. In order to take this oath, Avraham says to Eliezer, "Place now your hand under my thigh," a euphemism for the male organ. The Midrash offers several explanations for this practice, including one making use of the principle of effort justification:

Rabbi Berachia said: because this mitzvah [i.e., *bris milah* (circumcision)] was given to them through pain, it was most dear to them; as such, they would only swear upon this mitzvah.

In other words, the common practice was to swear by something that is precious, and Rabbi Berachia is describing why it was so precious to Avraham: the effort and pain that he went through to fulfill the *mitzvah*. As such, it was fitting to use the place of the *bris milah* as the object upon which Avraham took his oath. As shown by the examples of Chana and Avraham, the effort one puts into an activity makes it more valuable or dear to the individual. Although most contemporary studies look at the economic impact of effort justification or the IKEA effect, they seem to be identifying a similar principle highlighted by Chazal for thousands of years.

Remarkably, this psychological principle is also relevant in halachic passages in the Gemara. The Mishnah (*Bava Metzia* 38a) records a disagreement about what to do in a case in which someone deposits produce with someone else to safeguard, and the produce begins to spoil or is eaten by pests. Rabban Shimon ben Gamliel argues what seems to be the most economically advantageous position: the guardian should sell the produce before too much is lost, and hold the money for the owner. The majority opinion, however, argues that the guardian should not sell the produce.[147] The majority view, at first glance, is perplexing—why would we not allow the guardian to sell the produce, which would protect the assets of the owner? The Gemara cites Rav Kahana to address this question:

---

147. The Gemara cites a disagreement regarding the exact nature of the cases being described in the Mishnah. See *Tur* and *Beis Yosef, Choshen Mishpat* 292:15 regarding how we rule.

Rav Kahana says [that it is based on the principle]: A person prefers a *kav* (measure of volume) of his own produce to nine *kav* of another's produce.

Rashi[148] adds the following explanation:

The produce is dear to him since he toiled for it. As such, he prefers the *kav* that remains to the nine *kav* of others' that he could acquire with the money if his produce were sold [by the guardian].

According to Rav Kahana, the majority view in the Mishnah acknowledges that the owner will end up with less money if the guardian holds on it; nevertheless, because he worked for it, the produce is more valuable to him than many times more produce that were not the direct fruits of his own labor. According to Rashi, Rav Kahana is not saying that *ownership* of the item leads to it having greater value; it is the effort to produce it that leads to a person considering it more dear. A number of Acharonim[149] suggest that it is possible that if it is known that the fruit was not produced by the owner, and instead was itself purchased produce, the *halachah* would allow for the guardian to sell it because this principle would not apply.

Additional Perspectives in Chazal

As the examples above show, Chazal understood this psychological phenomenon very well, and considered it prominent enough to

---

148. Ramban in *Milchamos* suggests a similar explanation.
149. E.g., Rashash, *Porat Yosef, Mitzpeh Eitan.*

potentially sway a halachic ruling. However, Chazal's understanding of the power of this effect seems to go beyond what is found in contemporary scientific literature, suggesting an additional layer to this widely-found cognitive bias. I will present below examples of two aspects found in Chazal that give additional insight into the IKEA effect: first, some sources indicate that, in addition to adding value, one's own effort may be a form of establishing a sense of ownership over the item[150]; second, the value of effort is not limited to the actor's perception, but also has religious or metaphysical value as well.

The Gemara discusses the law of who has the rights to land's increased value—the seller's creditor or the buyer (*Bava Metzia* 14b). There are many permutations of the question, and discussing the complexities is beyond the scope of this chapter. However, Rav Chaim of Brisk, in his commentary on Rambam (*Hilchos Malveh ve-Loveh* 21:1), discusses the law of someone who plants seeds in land that is not his:

> ... even though it is explicit that one who trespasses into another's field [and plants seeds] the improvement belongs to the owner of the field, in a case that a person plants seeds in an ownerless field we do not say... that the improvements are ownerless; instead, everything [that was planted] belongs to the one who planted the seeds [even though the field remains ownerless].

---

150. Some researchers have connected the IKEA effect with the endowment effect or loss aversion on a theoretical basis, but I am unaware of studies that have shown them to be related.

In other words, Rav Chaim understands that the act of planting creates a bond of ownership over the produce that emerges as a result, even if there is no legal ownership bond with the land itself.[151]

The Gemara does not offer a source for this reasoning; however, one could suggest that this attitude, that one's labor creates a bond of ownership, emerges from a Biblical source. When Avraham returned from his miraculous successful military victory to save Lot, he was greeted by Malki-Tzedek, who offered a blessing: "Blessed be Avraham of God Most High, Creator [*koneh*] of heaven and earth" (*Bereishis* 14:19). Rashi, based on the Gemara,[152] notices the unusual word for Creator and comments:

> This is similar to the verse, "He who creates [*oseh*] heaven and earth" (*Tehillim* 134:3)—by making them, He acquired [*koneh*] them to belong to Him.

As Rashi explains, through making heaven and earth, God assumed ownership over them. This idea that God's toiling, so to speak, to create the universe, gives Him ownership over it, may be a foundation for Rav Chaim's *chiddush* (novel idea), that the one who plants seeds in an ownerless field has ownership over the produce.

IKEA and the Endowment Effect—Are They Related?

It is worth considering whether this approach emerging from the Gemara, that making something contributes to a sense of ownership,

---

151. For another example, see *Bava Metzia* 111b, regarding the *hava aminah* of withholding payment.

152. *Pesachim* 87b. A similar passage is found in *Pirkei Avos* (6:12); however, see Rashi there who says that the text in the Gemara seems more correct.

may provide an insight into the psychological mechanisms behind the IKEA effect. Three primary possible explanations have been suggested to explain the IKEA effect: "(1) signal of competence, (2) effort justification, and (3) mere ownership."[153] My focus here is on the final suggestion, that ownership over the item would lead to higher valuation, a well-known phenomenon known as the "endowment effect,"[154] which also has a basis in Talmudic texts.[155] Notably, both Norton (2012) and Marsh (2018) argue that their respective study's findings run counter to what would be expected if the endowment effect were the mechanism behind the IKEA effect. Norton, however, does not provide an explanation for why their findings are inconsistent with the endowment effect. In one part of Marsh's study, the researchers had young children make art projects at a museum, but informed the kids that they would not be able to bring the projects home; in this condition, students still valued their project more than other projects that they did not make. Marsh argues that their findings run counter to the endowment effect:

> Results from our study provide preliminary evidence against this claim as children still displayed a bias for their created items, compared to identical items, despite the lack

153. Marsh, L. E., Kanngiesser, P., & Hood, B. (2018). When and how does labour lead to love? The ontogeny and mechanisms of the IKEA effect. *Cognition, 170,* 245-253.

154. For a discussion of possible mechanisms driving the endowment effect, see Morewedge, C. K., & Giblin, C. E. (2015). Explanations of the endowment effect: an integrative review. *Trends in Cognitive Sciences, 19*(6), 339-348.

155. For example, see Rashi, *Shabbos* 10b, s.v. *milta albishei yakira.*

of explicit ownership labels.... While it is possible that children still experience feelings of ownership for their creation, even when told that they cannot take it home, we argue that denying children the opportunity to keep their object removes access, control and possession of it.

In other words, because the children were told that they may not bring the project home, the perception of ownership must not be present.

Both Norton and Marsh seem to assume that ownership, which is the basis for the endowment effect, is a binary question— either one owns something or one does not.[156] Some researchers have pointed out that this assumption may not be accurate, from a psychological perspective, instead suggesting that psychological ownership should be viewed across a spectrum[157] and can be influenced by a number of factors unrelated to legal ownership, such as touch, imagery, or creative design.[158] In contrast to Norton and Marsh, we could understand that building or creating an item leads to a psychological sense of ownership, legal or not, which, in turn, contributes to the higher valuation of the item compared to an item over which a person does not have a similar sense of psychological

---

156. Marsh does mention the idea of feelings of ownership, but they reject it as implausible in their study.

157. E.g., Reb, J., & Connolly, T. (2007). Possession, feelings of ownership, and the endowment effect. *Judgment and Decision Making, 2*(2), 107.

158. E.g., Shu, S. B., & Peck, J. (2011). Psychological ownership and affective reaction: Emotional attachment process variables and the endowment effect. *Journal of Consumer Psychology, 21*(4), 439-452.

ownership. Such an understanding may emerge from the from the Talmudic sources above. The planter of seeds, simply by virtue of his labor, is thought to have ownership bonds over the otherwise ownerless produce. Similarly, God is called the *koneh*, or Owner, of the universe, by virtue of His having created the universe. In each of these cases, the work or effort performed by either God or the laborer leads to a sense of ownership, which, based on the principle of the endowment effect, would in turn lead to increased valuation of the item.

This view, that one's toil in producing something leads to a sense of ownership is supported by another Rashi. The Gemara (*Avodah Zarah* 19a) records a number of *drashos* focusing on a verse in *Tehillim* (1:2) praising the righteous: "But his desire is in the Torah of Hashem, and in his Torah he meditates day and night." The simplest explanation of the verse is that "his Torah" should be read "His Torah," namely that the antecedent of the word "His" is Hashem, mentioned earlier in the verse. The Gemara, however, reads word "his" as referring to the righteous student engaged in Torah study:

And Rava also says, with regard to this verse: Initially the Torah is called by the name of the Holy One, Blessed be He, but ultimately it is called by the name of the one who studies it. As it is first stated: "His delight is in the Torah of the Lord," and in the continuation of the verse it states: "And in his Torah he meditates day and night."

Rashi explains the mechanism through which the student is thought to have acquired the Torah for himself: "The Torah is called by the name of the student who toiled in it." Rashi does not emphasize that the Torah is the possession of a person by virtue of his knowing it; instead, he highlights that it is specifically the effort that one puts in that brings about this sense of ownership. What seems to emerge from Rashi's commentary here, as well as his commentary in the other places listed above, is a consistent view that toiling on behalf of something both creates a bond of ownership, as well as a subjective increase in the value of the item.

Lesson for Today

I have had many conversations with people who share the following sentiment: "I wish I were more motivated, because if I had the motivation, I would do X." I have heard this comment regarding exercise, praying, dieting, studying, refraining from unwanted behavior, speaking more kindly to one's spouse, and other aspects of life. On its surface, this seems like an intuitive idea—why would I do something if I am not motivated to do it? The belief then forms that for them to change their behavior, they must first work on being motivated for the specific behavior, which will then lead to performing the behavior.

Part of my role as a psychotherapist is to challenge this belief that one cannot act in a certain way without feeling motivated. Not only does this belief sometimes serve as an impediment to making wanted changes in one's life, but the reality often works in opposite direction. When we practice certain behaviors, we come to value those behaviors more, which can serve to increase our motivation to continue those behaviors. Seen in this way, committed effort, not motivation, is the primary driver behind changing behaviors, as well as increasing the way we value the new behaviors and their outcomes.

In addition to the link between effort and our own subjective valuation of our actions, this phenomenon seems to be reflected by God as well. There is no shortage of statements in Rabbinic literature emphasizing the important of effort in the service of God, perhaps most succinctly put in *Pirkei Avos* (5:23): "Ben He He said: According to the labor is the reward." This statement declares that the Divine reward we receive depends on the degree of effort we put into something, and as described in the following passage, may suggest a moral imperative to increase our efforts in the service of God (*Sotah* 22a):

> The significance of receiving divine reward can be learned from a widow, as there was a certain widow in whose neighborhood there was a synagogue, and despite this every day she went and prayed in the study hall of Rabbi Yochanan. Rabbi Yochanan said to her: My daughter, is there not a synagogue in your neighborhood? She said to him: My teacher, don't I attain a reward for all the steps I take while walking to pray in the distant study hall?

Even though, all things being equal, praying in a study hall (*beis midrash*) is preferred to praying in a *shul* (*beis knesses*), Rabbi Yochanan still questions why this woman decided to walk to his study hall despite having a *shul* in her neighborhood. Rabbi

Yochanan accepts her reply, that she wants to receive reward for the effort walking to the *shul*, such that he challenges a teaching of Rebbi with this story of the woman, and the Gemara assumes that he adopted this woman's position as his own (*Bava Metzia* 107a).

This psychological mechanism, that exerting energy towards one's goals leads to one attributing greater value to those goals, is crucial to our own personal development and the education of our children. Of course, sometimes the instruction needs to start with the consideration of what we value, and how we should be motivated to act in accordance with those values. Nevertheless, as described in this chapter, the flip is also true. All of the *mussar shmoozen* [sermons] in the world about the lofty ideas fulfilled through sitting in a *sukkah* may not give a child the same connection to the mitzvah of *sukkah* than would building the *sukkah* for himself. In addition to writing a check to help poor people, as necessary as that is to helping those in need, to fully appreciate the mitzvah of *tzedakah* [giving charity] we may also cook dinner ourselves for someone who is hungry. This principle may be applied to religious activities, relationships with family and friends, recreational interests, and many other aspects of life. If we can do this for ourselves and our children, we can encourage a life of fulfillment and meaning that reflects the efforts that we put in.

Freedom Isn't Free

Combat-Related Moral Injury
in Torah and *Halachah* (32b)

לְכוּ נָא וְנִוָּכְחָה, יֹאמַר ד' אִם יִהְיוּ חֲטָאֵיכֶם
כַּשָּׁנִים כַּשֶּׁלֶג יַלְבִּינוּ אִם יַאְדִּימוּ כַתּוֹלָע כַּצֶּמֶר יִהְיוּ:

"Come now, and let us reason together, says the Lord; though your sins be as scarlet, they shall be as white as snow; though they be red like crimson, they shall be as wool" — Yeshayahu 1:18

As many scientists, journalists, politicians, and civilians can attest, the recent wars in Iraq, Afghanistan, and other battles fought in the Global War on Terrorism have been waged at tremendous cost to life and property. In addition to physical casualties and fatalities, the psychological impact on military service members and civilians has been enormous, and, among other advancements in the psychological understanding of returning combat veterans, researchers and clinicians have placed great emphasis on a concept referred to as "moral injury."

Defining Moral Injury

In the most comprehensive description of moral injury to date, Litz describes a phenomenon that includes impairment to psychological, emotional, spiritual, biological functioning resulting from "serious and/or sustained" exposure to experiences that violate their deeply held moral or ethical beliefs.[159] Defined in this way, exposure to a morally injurious event can be seen as either distinct from, or under the umbrella of, exposure to a traumatic event, a category that has received much greater attention in contemporary scientific literature. According to a relatively narrow definition specified by the most recent psychiatric diagnostic manual,[160] a traumatic event is one that includes exposure to "death, threatened death, actual or threatened serious injury, or actual or threatened sexual violence"; this exposure can be direct, or through witnessing in person, learning about threat to a loved one, or repeated direct exposure to the aversive details. This definition places events that are purely moral in nature outside the realm of "trauma." However, the perspective of most clinicians is that trauma should entail a broader definition that includes any event that violates one's belief in the normal way of the world, and overwhelms one's ability to cope. Understood in this way, morally injurious events are well within the world of trauma.

Of course, moral injury, as a phenomenon, is not new. Intrinsic to human nature, it would appear, is a vulnerability to severe violations of one's moral code. In recent years, psychiatrists and

159. Litz, B. T., Stein, N., Delaney, E., Lebowitz, L., Nash, W. P., Silva, C., & Maguen, S. (2009). Moral injury and moral repair in war veterans: A preliminary model and intervention strategy. *Clinical Psychology Review, 29*(8), 695-706.

160. American Psychiatric Association. (2013). *Diagnostic and statistical manual of mental disorders* (5th ed.). Arlington, VA: Author.

psychologists have drawn attention to this injury suffered by military members who have faced combat; one such psychiatrist has drawn parallels between the experiences of contemporary warriors with the betrayals depicted in Homer's epic poems.[161] It should not be surprising, then, that in the sea of classical Jewish literature we find reflections of these universal principles of moral injury, legalistic applications of exposure to morally injurious experiences, and instruction for how to achieve repair.

An aspect of moral injury that is distinct from other types of trauma is that modern psychologists tend to consider moral injury an outcome of war, and not of other contexts; nevertheless, for the serious Jewish thinker, there is another relevant, universal word for this: "sin." Careful observance of the commandments is the path to a relationship with God, perhaps man's most lofty goal, and violating this code leads to a severance in that relationship (*Yeshayahu* 59:2). From time immemorial, the Torah and Midrash have described the trauma of perpetrating sin and its devastating eternal impact: Adam and Chava violating God's first commandment; Cain murdering Hevel in cold blood; Yaakov's sons conspiring to sell Yosef; and perhaps most potent, the sin of the golden calf. Each of these events, and others in the Bible, carried with it a Divine punishment, but more relevant for us, the Midrash describes the personal and national psychological and spiritual devastation following the perpetration. The weight of self-awareness of perpetration is overwhelming, a

---

161. Shay, J., Cleland, M., & McCain, J. (2003). *Odysseus in America: Combat trauma and the trials of homecoming.* Simon and Schuster.

crushing burden.[162] The perpetration is constantly on one's mind,[163] and one feels ashamed,[164] unable to face God or fellow man.

Surely, even those not well versed in Jewish law can perceive a violation of their moral code. Indeed, universal ethical principles and moral codes exist, and violation of these codes is meaningful beyond their implications in terms of sin or transgressions.[165] In the course of warfare, we can imagine many opportunities to confront potential violations such as killing, harming, or failing to protect others, especially civilians; destruction or theft of property when unrelated to the goals of combat; being harmed by someone else engaging in these behaviors; or perhaps even witnessing these violations occurring.

Before limiting my focus to the overlap of psychological and Torah literature, it is important for context to make two observations. The first relates to how this discussion fits in to the history of warfare, because, as noted above, warfare and its moral implications are not unique to the modern era as studied by contemporary psychology, nor is it unique to those bound by *halachah*. Verkamp, a contemporary philosopher,[166] traced the history of reintegration of Christian soldiers after their return from warfare, which often

162. *Torah Sheleimah, Bereishis* 4:106 (volume 2).

163. *Tehillim* 51:5: "My sin is ever before me."

164. *Yirmiyahu* 3:25: "Let us lie down in our shame, and let our confusion cover us; for we have sinned against the Lord, our God... and we have not hearkened to the voice of the Lord our God."

165. For an eloquent presentation of these ideas, see Rabbi Aharon Lichtenstein's *Leaves of Faith*, vol. 2, pp. 102-123.

166. Verkamp, B. J. (1988). Moral Treatment of Returning Warriors in the Early Middle Ages. *The Journal of Religious Ethics*, 223-249.

involved extended periods of penance. These practices, which span from the earliest days of Christianity until after the Reformation,[167] account for the ever-present opportunity for sin during combat. As Verkamp records, the most severe penance was required in the case of killing others, with some variation in the penance requirement depending on intent; this requirement highlights that for the theologians in charge of providing reintegration guidelines to their troops, the act of killing another person reflects a severe sin, to some extent, in any context. Other sins, such as "cowardice, anger, pride, avarice, sloth," also required various acts of penance; each of these were meant to be evaluated as returning warriors sought to reintegrate into their communities. In contemporary language, we might say that these soldiers had exposure to potentially morally injurious events, and their religious leaders provided prescribed guidelines, within their context, for achieving moral repair.

This discussion of the history of moral violations in combat leads directly to the second notable point. From a psychological perspective, moral injury, as I am presenting it here, may be only tangentially related to what a person "should" feel in the course of battle, from the perspective of morality or the ethics of war. One can imagine a dedicated and conscientious warrior who, despite attacking only those who presented a threat to him or fellow troops, is bothered by the reality that he killed other people. Similarly, one may encounter a fighter who purposely killed non-threatening civilians in a fit of rage and remains unbothered by his actions.

167. Kelle, B. E. (2014). Postwar rituals of return and reintegration. *Warfare, Ritual, and Symbol in Biblical and Modern Contexts, 18,* 205.

Endless distinctions can be made about how culpable a fighter is, from a moral view, in any act of war that causes damage to people or property: did he have intent for his action; was there a direct order; was there more information to be gathered before a strike; could he have safely hesitated to evaluate the situation more carefully; did he ensure all the safety procedures were followed; was the context of the battle forcing his hand; did he engage with malice; etc. All of these interplaying dimensions, and others, provide fascinating philosophical questions, with a profound impact on psychological issues. Nevertheless, as with many cases, the psychological and emotional impact of morally injurious events does not necessarily attend to philosophical nuance.[168] For this reason, I will not discuss the "should" or "should not" of wartime morality, but rather draw from sources that study what is, and how Torah and *halachah* shed light on those realities. It is in this context that I will discuss several types of what is referred to as "potentially morally injurious events."

Categories of Morally Injurious Events

To appreciate the nature of each type of potentially morally injurious event, I will offer excerpts or vignettes that reflect actual stories and experiences reported by combat veterans.

---

168. The philosophical distinctions do play a role in psychotherapeutic interventions. For example, one of the gold standard approaches to treating post-traumatic stress, "Cognitive Processing Therapy," relies heavily on helping the patient place his actions in context to reduce moral culpability. But for many combat veterans, weighing the nuance of one's actions through a moral or philosophical lens is a skill that needs to be developed, and is not immediately present.

Perpetration

Quang Ngai and Quang Nam are provinces in central Vietnam, between the mountains and the sea. Ken Kerney, William Doyle and Rion Causey tell horrific stories about what they saw and did there as soldiers in 1967. That spring and fall, American troops conducted operations there to engage the enemy and drive peasants out of villages and into heavily guarded "strategic hamlets." The goal was to deny the Viet Cong support, shelter, and food. The fighting was intense and the results, the former soldiers say, were especially brutal. Villages were bombed, burned and destroyed. As the ground troops swept through, in many cases they gunned down men, women and children, sometimes mutilating bodies—cutting off ears to wear on necklaces. They threw hand grenades into dugout shelters, often killing entire families.[169]

"Thou shalt not murder" is one of the most well-known verses of the Bible, which prohibits the most impactful, most irreversible act that a person can perpetrate against another. While Jewish and secular laws sanction *killing* others in some circumstances, and war always entails the use of lethal force to protect one's interests, the universal prohibition of *murder* is well understood. For warriors, violations of this prohibition can take the form of being responsible for the death of enemies, bystanders or civilians, or allies. Obviously, for those associated with deceased, this event is catastrophic. But for the perpetrator as well, the act of killing itself may be life-altering, a categorical shift: *before I was a person who had not taken another*

---

169. Report on Brutal Vietnam Campaign Stirs Memories, *New York Times*, Dec. 28, 2003. Retrieved from: http://www.nytimes.com/2003/12/28/us/report-on-brutal-vietnam-campaign-stirs-memories.html?pagewanted=all

life and now, I am a killer. This recognition that one has cut short another's life, the gravity of which may only be realized over time, can lead to the most piercing and devastating existential questions.[170] Indeed, the *Or ha-Chaim* (*Devarim* 13:18) understands Hashem's promise to the Jewish people who exact capital punishment on the "wayward city"—that Hashem "will give you mercy and be merciful to you"—as a way to combat the negative psychological impact of carrying out such an act.

The psychological trauma of killing another person is surely amplified if the killing is not justified and not within the scope of the mission. In the heat of the moment, soldiers may find themselves in a dissociated state, numb to the norms of human morality, and commit acts that reflect the height of cruelty and barbarism. But over time, as the memories of their behavior clash with their returning sense of humanity, and the dissonance between their beliefs and their behavior, their moral compass and their malice, becomes torturous.

---

170. Recent psychological research has highlighted the profound impact of killing others in combat. See, for example, Maguen, S., Luxton, D. D., Skopp, N. A., Gahm, G. A., Reger, M. A., Metzler, T. J., & Marmar, C. R. (2011). Killing in combat, mental health symptoms, and suicidal ideation in Iraq war veterans. *Journal of Anxiety Disorders,* 25(4), 563-567; see also Maguen, S., Lucenko, B. A., Reger, M. A., Gahm, G. A., Litz, B. T., Seal, K. H., ... & Marmar, C. R. (2010). The impact of reported direct and indirect killing on mental health symptoms in Iraq war veterans. *Journal of Traumatic Stress,* 23(1), 86-90. A particularly powerful example in halachic literature can be found in Minchas Yitzchak 6:55, who discusses a case of a Holocaust survivor who feels guilty decades later for causing the death of a Jewish kapo who was beating other prisoners by turning him in to the Nazi officers.

The abundance of statements in classical Jewish literature relating to the inestimable value of human life only intensifies the devastation. A single person is compared to the value of a whole world (*Sanhedrin* 37a), and saving a life takes precedence over violation of nearly all the other commandments (*Sanhedrin* 74a). Even in battling enemies, as the Midrash describes, both Avraham[171] and Yaakov[172] feared that they may have killed, or may be forced to kill improperly in the course of battle. Indeed, God Himself is portrayed as demonstrating concern and sadness even for the death of the Egyptians at the Sea of Reeds, despite their collective, cruel enslavement of the Israelites for hundreds of years (*Megillah* 10b).

Perhaps the most illuminating example of the qualitative change that occurs when someone takes another life is seen in the case of the killing priest. The priest, by definition, is a direct descendent of Aaron who is characterized as someone who "loved and pursued peace" (*Pirkei Avos* 1:12). As such, the priest is charged with being a representative of the Jewish people to God, as well as a conduit for God's blessing of peace to the Jewish people (*Bamidbar* 6:27). The Gemara (*Berachos* 32), based on *Yeshayahu* 1:15, concludes that a priest who has murdered another person is permanently prohibited from offering this blessing of peace (*Shulchan Aruch, Orach Chaim* 128:35); he, the priest, is forever changed, and even repentance may not repair the damage.[173] The

---

171. *Bereishis Rabbah* 44; cited in *Torah Sheleimah, Bereishis* 15:10.
172. Cited in Rashi, *Bereishis* 32:8.
173. *Mishnah Berurah*, ad loc. In some cases he may regain the ability through repentance, such as accidental causation of death, or not lose the right at all, such as completely involuntary killing without neglect.

murderer's hands which wrought such havoc and destruction are contaminated, disqualified from serving as a vehicle to deliver a divine blessing.[174] How can a person be a pursuer and lover of peace when his hands are full of blood?

Warriors in just wars battle to preserve peace and security for those they protect; they use lethal force against enemies who seek to harm them or their citizens. How do these two roles co-exist? To some degree, for some individuals, they cannot. The memories of killing another person are seared on his mind, frustrating his attempts to rise above them and become an agent of peace. He has been transformed, and he thinks he has lost the ability, or even the right, to bring joy and peace to the world, by virtue of cutting another's life short, especially if he has caused the death of a civilian or incapacitated combatant. Despite the gravity of his circumstances, several aspects of Jewish law provide a window of relief. First, even in the case of the killing priest, if he killed in the context of a legal war he is not disqualified; instead, his actions are commendable as he has acted justly to protect the innocent.[175] A second aspect to

---

174. *Mishnah Berurah*, s.v. *ein kategor na'aseh sanigor.*

175. While a complete discussion of the issue is beyond the scope of this chapter, it is important to note that the *halachah* in this instance is not simple. Each aspect of the topic is controversial, with disagreements spanning the Rishonim through contemporary *poskim*, with controversy regarding the nature of prohibition (Torah-level prohibition or Rabbinic stringency); is accidental (*shogeg*) different than intentional (*meizid*) and does *teshuvah* matter in either instance; is a case of being compelled (*oness*) distinct from accidental; are gentiles who do not observe the seven Noahide laws included in the prohibition; and to what extent fighting in particular wars qualify as a mitzvah. See *Yechaveh*

consider is that even though a priest, with his unique stature, cannot reverse the clocks entirely with his repentance, Jewish law teaches that repentance is appropriate for everyone.[176] Despite the great and everlasting damage one has caused through the murder of another, God guarantees that He will attend to one's sincere attempts of repentance and grant some degree of atonement.

Aftermath of Battle

Even for those who are not directly involved in violent acts, moral injury may result of exposure to the great desolation brought about by war.

> M. is a big man; in addition to his personal weapon and gear he carried machine gun ammunition and the PRC-25 radio long distances in many patrols in the triple canopy jungle near L. Because he was big he was told to carry the battalion's first kill, the body of a dead Viet Cong with half his head blown off, back to the landing zone so the company commander could verify the body count. After three days of the putrefying body fluids and brain

Da'as 2:17 and Rabbi Gedaliah Felder's *Yesodei Yeshurun*, Chelek 2, page 51. See also *Techumin* 6 page 31 at length. Despite this multi-dimensional controversy, most contemporary *poskim* agree that a *kohen* who kills in the course of a justified battle is eligible to recite the priestly blessings. See *Igros Moshe, Yoreh De'ah* 2:158 at the end; a similar idea is found in *Zohar* 3:214 brought in *Torah Sheleimah, Bamidbar* 13:115.

176. *Chagigah* 15a. As noted in the introduction, a complete discussion of *teshuvah*, including the various levels of incomplete *teshuvah*, is well beyond the scope of this chapter.

matter dripping on him, the CO. did not show up and he was ordered to dump the body in a riverbed. M. cannot get the taste of putrefaction out of his mouth and nose.[177]

Among the most distressing parts of war is the aftermath of battle, when survivors come into contact with the vast carnage that has transpired. Life feels cheap (*Tehillim* 44:12), maybe pointless (*Iyov* 7:16), and those who were killed were given no regard; perhaps the survivor is tormented while the dead are at peace! In truth, even enemy death has an impact. Imagine the rage and desire for revenge one may feel towards one's enemy, as the Jews might have toward the Egyptians following the latter's demise in the Sea of Reeds.[178] Or the existential despair of quiet reflection on the impact on the enemies' families and communities, their deaths so easily caused yet the effects so burdensome for their loved ones. Indeed, the 100 shofar blasts on Rosh Hashanah, one of Judaism's most sacred rituals, commemorates the crying of Sisra's mother awaiting her son's return when he was killed in battle with the Israelites (*Rosh Hashanah* 33b).

Surely the death of friends, with all the feelings of loss, mourning, sadness and fear, is incalculably worse. These universal and eternal reactions are laid out in remarkable poignancy and detail in the book of *Iyov*. If one believes in God, he may struggle with the belief in God's fairness, or God's existence entirely. For a non-believer, perhaps the world looks like an increasingly cruel place. To experience this despair he need not have guilt—indeed, one can feel blameless, yet still despise life after experiencing such vast death.

---

177. Shay, J. (1991). Learning about combat stress from Homer's Iliad. *Journal of Traumatic Stress, 4*(4), 561-579.

178. See *Torah Sheleimah, Parashas Beshalach* #202.

To some degree, this reaction is desired and admirable—what kind of person remains unmoved and undisturbed after an encounter with death and suffering! Even God Himself, as it were, is viewed as being aggrieved upon the death of a person justly condemned to capital punishment (*Sanhedrin* 46a). A person who is not disturbed rejects a basic appreciation of human dignity, and denies the fundamental belief that man was created in the image of God. Indeed, Rabbi Meir famously presents a parable of twins, one who was appointed king, and another who became a highway robber. The latter was caught and executed, and a passerby who saw him hanging would exclaim: "The king is hanged!" Thus, in interpreting the mitzvah to hang someone who has been stoned, the Gemara instructs that "one ties [the deceased] up and another unties [him]" (*Sanhedrin* 46b)—in other words, although the Torah requires him to be hanged, the deceased is hanged for the least amount of time possible out of respect for his basic human dignity.

Despite the fundamental belief in the incalculable value of man, a person who remains mired in sorrow, who mourns excessively, negates an acceptance of God's divine justice (*Moed Katan* 27b). In response to this sensitivity to human dignity, as well as human death and suffering, and perhaps to help mitigate the extreme anguish contact with death and suffering may cause, Jewish law has codified a number of rituals. When one is present as a person's soul departs, he must rend his clothing, but tearing clothing outside of this requirement is considered wasteful and inappropriate. We desist from our normal activities for the week of *shiva* (mourning), but still Jews in general, and priests especially, are exhorted to not mourn excessively. A full discussion of how *halachah* and psychology approach recovering one's sense of human dignity through mourning and grief rituals is beyond the scope of this chapter.[179] Nevertheless, appreciating the deleterious effect of encountering extreme death through both psychology and *halachah* can provide a useful starting point for moving forward.

Betrayal

In some cases, severe violations of one's moral or ethical codes may not involve a direct encounter with death.

> The actions of an inexperienced officer put the rest of the patrol in serious danger during the course of the patrol. The anger was palpable to say the least when the boys got back to camp. What has made the situation worse over the years...was that the officer concerned falsified the reports of the events that took place and caused a number of (disability) claims to be denied as the traumatic incident... was at odds with the "official report." Many of the claimants were shattered to find an officer had lied to cover his own shortcomings. There was at least one attempted suicide—thankfully unsuccessful.[180]

179. For a more complete view, see Spero, M. H. (1977). Halakhah as psychology: Explicating the laws of mourning. *Tradition: A Journal of Orthodox Jewish Thought, 17*(1), 173-184. For some additional perspective, see also Wahlhaus, E. (2005). The Psychological benefits of the traditional Jewish mourning rituals: Have the changes instituted by the Progressive Movement enhanced or diminished Them?. *European Judaism, 38*(1), 95-109.

180. McCormack, L., & Joseph, S. (2014). Psychological growth in aging Vietnam veterans redefining shame and betrayal. *Journal of Humanistic Psychology, 54*(3), 336-355.

The nature of warfare requires warriors to place enormous faith in one another, as one must trust his partner to fight courageously to protect himself and his squad. For those who have not fought in combat, it is difficult to appreciate the depth of the relationships forged among allies in battle. Who knows how many times a soldier's life is saved due to the actions of his friends, and how many others' lives he saved through his own performance. Indeed, Jewish law maintains that people with qualities that impose barriers to this trust are disqualified from serving in the military, as it would put the entire military enterprise at risk (*Devarim* 20:3-7).

Imagine the psychological devastation a service member must feel, then, when he discovers his fellow warrior has failed to uphold the military code. The person for whom you would die on the battlefield has shown no regard for your commitment to him and your sacrifice, instead choosing his own needs above the group's, be they for personal gain or temporary relief through impetuous reactions.

Perhaps the best example of military betrayal in the Bible involved Achan in the book of *Yehoshua*. The Israelites were finally entering Canaan, and they conquered Yericho with clear divine assistance. In their victory, Yehoshua commanded the army against plundering Yericho (chapter 7); unbeknownst to Yehoshua or the rest of *B'nei Yisrael*, Achan disobeyed this order and stole loot from the conquered city. Simply put, because of Achan's failure, soldiers died. His actions caused a removal of God's protection from the Jewish people (see Malbim on *Yehoshua* 7:1), and they suffered a devastating defeat in their next battle, as they lost 36 fighters and were forced to flee. The Rabbis attribute a host of negative traits to

Achan (*Sanhedrin* 43b-44a), all a reflection of how negatively they viewed his betrayal.

Contemporary warriors are not afforded knowledge of God's favor, but acts and feelings of betrayal are no less present. As with Achan, fellow service members can fail to live up to expectations, which may lead to the death or injury of friends. An officer may act capriciously, which jeopardizes the lives of those who serve under him, and civilian leaders may make politically motivated decisions that violate the trust of military members. Betrayal shatters trust, and destroys one's ability to have reliance on others.

Impact of Moral Injury

Moral Injury as a Trauma

Psychologists do not yet know the full range of psychological, emotional, biological, and spiritual impact of moral injury. However, many agree to the extent that moral injury results from a traumatic event, as defined above; those who suffer from moral injury will likely share symptoms with those who suffer from other traumatic events. One of the signature challenges faced by trauma survivors is avoidance of reminders of the trauma. Take, for example, this comment from a testimonial of an individual who helped liberate Dachau: "The Jewish people and all the rest of us should continue to try to encourage all of us to remember places like Dachau—*despite my own constant push to repress that which is so horrible,* I too would like to forget but I can't quite cut it."[181]

---

181. Retrieved from http://remember.org/witness/belcher.

This pattern of avoidance following a morally injurious event was noted roughly two thousand years ago. On the final day of consecration of the *mishkan* in the wilderness, Moshe was transferring the priestly duties to Aharon and his sons. Finally, after the catastrophic sin of the golden calf, in which Aharon was involved, the Jewish people and Aharon had been granted atonement and the priestly service would bring God's presence to tabernacle. In giving Aharon the instructions, Moshe urged him to "approach the altar and perform [your offerings]" (*Vayikra* 9:7). Why did Aharon need to be encouraged to approach the altar—was he hesitant? Targum Yonatan explains that in approaching the altar, Aharon saw its "horns"—the posts at each corner that extend above altar's level. Aharon was jolted, ashamed, cautious and afraid; these horns, in language and form, were reminiscent, for him, of the horns of the golden calf. Was he deserving of being the high priest, of performing a service on behalf of the Jewish people? He shied away. To this reaction, Moshe responded to him to fear not; he reminded Aharon that God had granted him forgiveness, and he need not shrink from this responsibility for which he was chosen (Ramban). Indeed, he had sinned; but through God's mercy he was forgiven and could serve as the liaison between God and His people.

In contemporary times, this pattern of avoidance can be seen commonly among combat veterans. One soldier who fired on a family cannot spend time around crying children; another will not engage with others to develop committed, loving relationships, because he expects to be betrayed; a third removes all sources of sensual pleasures from his life, as those who perished cannot share in this joy. In each of these instances, and the diverse cases experienced in combat, the avoidance is not due to a fear-based life-threat event, which is typically associated with avoidance. Instead, it is due to the activation of distressing memories conditioned to be paired with these moral violations, which are themselves coupled with painful emotions.

Emotions of Moral Injury #1: Shame and Guilt

As anyone who has dealt with intense emotion can attest, defining the exact experience of any emotion is difficult, and distinguishing between two similar emotions, such as shame and guilt, is particularly challenging. Compounding the problem in regard to shame and guilt is the inconsistency among researchers of how to operationalize and measure these constructs,[182] beyond their generic classification as "social-moral emotions." Although psychologists generally accept that lay-people and clinicians alike use these terms interchangeably, researchers have found important, if subtle distinctions between the emotions of shame and guilt. Perhaps the most significant difference is that shame involves a stronger focus on the self—"*I* did that horrible thing"—while guilt involves a stronger focus on the behavior—"I *did* that horrible *thing*."[183]

In the case of a morally injurious event, the index offense may be viewed as interpersonal in nature through violating one's relationship

---

182. Blum, A. (2008). Shame and guilt, misconceptions and controversies: A critical review of the literature. *Traumatology, 14*(3), 91.

183. Tangney, J. P., Stuewig, J., & Mashek, D. J. (2007). Moral emotions and moral behavior. *Annual Review of Psychology, 58*, 345; Tangney, J. P. (1996). Conceptual and methodological issues in the assessment of shame and guilt. *Behaviour Research and Therapy, 34*, 741-754.

with God or man. Emotion researchers, such as Baumeister, have observed that this type of offense is particularly suited to engender feelings of guilt, which is viewed as a more pro-social emotion than shame.[184] Shame, on the other hand, may lead to a tendency to retreat or escape from others. This distinction leads to a generally accepted position that experiencing guilt has more benefits than experiencing shame. Nevertheless, others consider guilt and shame to be synonymous, at least on a practical level.[185]

Whichever definition of guilt and shame one accepts, the recognition that one has transgressed his moral code in a severe way provokes a reaction of embarrassment, shame, and guilt, whether one has religious sensitivities or not (see *Shaarei Teshuvah* 1:22). But for those who take stock of their religious performance, falling short of God's expectations carries additional weight. Consider this passage in the Yom Kippur liturgy, after reciting a complete confession of sins we transgressed and those we did not,[186] we recite the following self-reflection:

---

184. Baumeister, R. F., Stillwell, A. M., & Heatherton, T. F. (1994). Guilt: an interpersonal approach. *Psychological Bulletin, 115,* 243.

185. For a review, see Kim, S., Thibodeau, R., & Jorgensen, R. S. (2011). Shame, guilt, and depressive symptoms: a meta-analytic review. *Psychological Bulletin,137*(1), 68. This ambiguity can be seen through cutting-edge brain research, as an fMRI study revealed guilt and shame share some parallel neural pathways and differ in others. See Michl, P., Meindl, T., Meister, F., Born, C., Engel, R. R., Reiser, M., & Hennig-Fast, K. (2014). Neurobiological underpinnings of shame and guilt: a pilot fMRI study. *Social Cognitive and Affective Neuroscience, 9*(2), 150-157.

186. See *Sefer Ha-Chasidim* chapter 601 for explanations for why we confess sins we did not commit.

My Lord, before I was created I was unworthy, and now that I am created it is as if I had not been created. I am dust in my life; how much more so in my death. Indeed, before You I am like a vessel filled with shame and disgrace.

Emotional reactions of shame and guilt to transgression are considered proper, even necessary.[187] Indeed, the lack of shame indicates a shallowness of deliberation and superficiality of the recognition of moral violations, and the prophets reprimand people for not feeling shame due to their actions (e.g., *Yirmiyahu* 6:15). In some regard, the discomfort of the experience of these emotions is itself a type of penance and provides atonement (*Berachos* 12), and also serves as a deterrent against sinning in the future.[188]

Nevertheless, excessive guilt or shame that would hinder repentance is seen negatively. One's obligation to perform *mitzvos* certainly does not cease with the performance of a sin, no matter how grave—quite the opposite! This point is emphasized by Rabbeinu Yonah regarding the statement "do not be wicked in your own eyes" (*Pirkei Avos* 2:13). He writes:

"He should not be wicked in his own eyes" such that he cannot repent. [If he does so], he has given up hope of repentance and if a sin confronts him it [will be as if the sin] is permissible, because he will think that this sin is minor compared to the severe sin that he had previously transgressed.

---

187. See *Orchos Tzaddikim, Sha'ar Ha-Bushah* for elaboration on the benefits of shame.

188. *Divrei Yirmiyahu* on Rambam, *Hilchos Teshuvah* 2:8.

An irredeemable sinner will view any additional sin as trivial. Indeed, prayer itself becomes inconsequential, as there is no hope for God's forgiveness.[189] As such, to whatever extent one's regret, shame and guilt interfere with instead of inspire, the perpetrator's emotions are excessive. Perhaps this tension between experiencing guilt and shame on the one hand, and not becoming entrapped in despair on the other, is reflected in the following disagreement (*Yoma* 86b):

> Our Rabbis taught: As for the sins which one has confessed on one Day of Atonement, he should not confess them on another Day of Atonement... and if he had not committed them again, yet confessed them again, then it is with regard to him that Scripture says: "As a dog that returns to his vomit, so is a fool that repeats his folly." Rabbi Eleazar ben Yaakov said: He is the more praiseworthy, as it is said: "For I know my transgressions, and my sin is even before me."

According the first opinion, little is to be gained by revisiting the ugliness of the sin;[190] once we have identified and purged ourselves from the sin, we need not ingest the putrid residue that might linger. This fixation on our old, terrible ways will impede our ability to move forward in the proper way. The perpetrator can move on. On the other hand, if we cannot revisit our misdeeds occasionally, what lessons can we really have learned? It is noteworthy that even

---

189. *Markeves ha-Mishnah*, ad loc.
190. This reading is consistent with the Talmud Yerushalmi, which asserts that one should regard previous sins as ones he had committed but for which he had been forgiven. A Midrash cited by *Mitzpeh Eitan* has an alternate read.

according to Rabbi Eleazar, this *viddui* (confession) should probably only take place once a year on Yom Kippur, not continuously.

Emotions of Moral Injury #2: Anger

If we are supposed to apply exacting standards to our own actions, how are we meant to relate to the behaviors of others? When a person suffers a betrayal at the hands of a leader or fellow warrior, it is understandable that anger follow betrayal. Perhaps as a cover for feeling intensely vulnerable, or perhaps as a reaction to betraying one's trust, rage becomes the emotional expression of being disappointed by those in whose hands he placed his life. As such, psychologists see anger as a double-edged sword: adaptive in some ways and destructive in others.[191]

In contrast to the positive spin some psychologists put on anger, *Chazal* saw anger in an exceedingly negative light, with almost entirely damaging outcomes. Certainly, the Sages recognized the ubiquity of circumstances that can lead to anger, and despite that instructed that a person should train himself to not become enraged even if situations are suited for anger (Rambam, *Hilchos De'os* 2:3). Someone who becomes enraged is viewed as someone engaged in idolatry, while someone who does not become angry is considered to be beloved by God (*Pesachim* 113b).

Surely, this standard is nearly impossibly high, as even Moses himself, identified as the most humble man to walk the earth (*Bamidbar* 12:3), failed to achieve perfection in this regard; as a result, he forgot previously learned laws and acted too impatiently

---

191. E.g., Wyer Jr, R. S., & Srull, T. K. (1993). *Perspectives on anger and emotion: Advances in social cognition* (Vol. 6). Hillsdale, NJ: Lawrence, Erlbaum.

with the Jewish people (*Vayikra Rabbah* 13:1). It is important to note that combining the ease with which many people can become angry and the severity of the situations that military fighters face with the negative view *halachah* has on anger, when one does become angry this experience can serve as another source of shame and guilt.

Emotions of Moral Injury #3: Contamination

Another reaction commonly associated with severe violations of moral codes is that of contamination.[192] Psychological research has demonstrated that this is true both in the instance of perpetration[193] as well as betrayal,[194] and this intense, negative feeling can feel overwhelming for warriors returning from battle. In some ways, this reaction to moral injury is the most pernicious. The contaminated person is a source of evil, not just an observer, and he may feel that the rot, which he has spread to others through his actions, cannot be cleansed.

One feels dirty, unable to rinse off the stench and rot caused by the misdeed, as described in the book of *Iyov* (9:30-31):

---

192. The history of feelings of contamination following battle and warfare, and rituals to purify from that contamination, is quite rich. See, for example, Smith, D. L., & Panaitiu, I. (2016). Horror Sanguinis. *Common Knowledge, 22*(1), 69-80, which outlines rituals from ancient and medieval Middle East and Europe, as well as Native American and African cultures.

193. Rachman, S., Radomsky, A. S., Elliott, C. M., & Zysk, E. (2012). Mental contamination: The perpetrator effect. *Journal of Behavior Therapy and Experimental Psychiatry, 43*(1), 587-593.

194. Rachman, S. (2010). Betrayal: A psychological analysis. *Behaviour Research and Therapy, 48*(4), 304-311.

Even if I washed myself with soap, and my hands with cleansing powder, You would plunge me into a slime pit so that even my clothes would detest me.

An examination of Biblical language reinforces this reaction to violating one's moral code. Certainly in the case of violation of sexual ethics, the Torah uses the word *tamei*, the same as for ritual impurity.[195] But this characterization extends to other sins as well, such as idolatry and mistreating the holy temple,[196] and perhaps even murder (*Tehillim* 106:38-39).[197]

This experience of sin as a contaminant is reflected in a custom that has developed, aimed at purification. Typically, a *mikveh* (ritual immersion pool) is used to purify oneself from ritual impurity as commanded in the Torah. However, when the Sages over the generations have sought ways to rid themselves of the feeling of spiritual contamination beyond the process of confession and repentance, the *mikveh* took on an additional role. According to some authorities, the practice of immersion on the eve of Rosh Hashanah and Yom Kippur[198] is to cleanse oneself from the dirtying spiritual effects of sinful behavior; this process has been coined *tevilah lesheim teshuvah*—immersion for the sake of repentance.[199]

---

195. See cases of Dinah, as well as the *sotah*.

196. See *Yechezkel* 5:11 and 9:7, as well as Radak to *Yechezkel* 22:3.

197. For more on this topic see Klawans, J. (2004). *Impurity and sin in ancient Judaism*. Oxford University Press and Büchler, A. (1967). *Studies in sin and atonement in the Rabbinic literature of the first century*. Ktav Pub. House. See also Rambam, *Moreh Nevuchim* 3:47.

198. Rema in *Shulchan Aruch* 581:4.

199. See *Mishneh Halachos*, vol. 12, *siman* 318, for an extensive discussion and sources.

Other punishments, such as exile, are viewed as a way of cleansing oneself from this spiritual filth (*Yechezkel* 22:15 and Malbim there), in addition to being a form of atonement (*Sanhedrin* 37b).

Lesson for Today

For psychotherapists, working with combat veterans who have experienced exposure to morally injurious events can test the limits of a therapist's skillset. Particularly among those with training in cognitive-behavioral therapy techniques, a common strategy is to help the client contextualize an event, which helps reduce the level of responsibility or shame a person attributes to himself following a misdeed. But some veterans do not accept absolution through contextualizing—his belief may be unchangeable that just because war is an awful pressure cooker, that does not diminish the terrible nature of his unjustifiable actions. The typical cognitive techniques may prove to be insufficient to provide relief from the internal pressure resulting from actions taken or witnessed in warfare.

So how does one help a person experiencing moral injury? For the most part, I did not address above what may be the most important aspect of the study of moral injury: moral repair. Generally speaking, the process of moral repair, including recent, cutting-edge moral injury treatments,[200] shares many similarities to the process of *teshuva*, or repentance. Compare the following formulations:

---

200. Gray, M. J., Schorr, Y., Nash, W., Lebowitz, L., Amidon, A., Lansing, A., ... & Litz, B. T. (2012). Adaptive disclosure: An open trial of a novel exposure-based intervention for service members with combat-related psychological stress injuries. *Behavior Therapy*, 43(2), 407-415.

Litz, 2009	Rambam, *Hilchos Teshuvah* 1:1
Self-forgiveness conceptually entails acknowledging the event, accepting responsibility for it, experiencing the negative emotions associated with it, devoting sufficient energy to heal, and committing to living differently in the future.	How does one confess? He says, "I beg of You, God, I have erred, been iniquitous, and willfully sinned before You, and performed such-and-such misdeed. I am remorseful and embarrassed of my actions, and I will never return to this behavior again"

In both instances, the perpetrator must have cognitive awareness of the transgression, appreciate its severity as evidenced by an emotional response, and resolve and take steps to avoid similar behavior in the future. Given this overlap in understanding the foundations of the process of repair, a deep understanding of *teshuva* surely would elucidate the process of moral repair. However, as countless pages have been written over the generations about *teshuvah*, fully appreciating the relationship of *teshuva* and repair for moral injury requires its own essay.

Perhaps the most fundamental lesson to emerge from an appreciation of moral injury is the necessity of the civilian population to be compassionate toward returning combat veterans. Some returning warriors have an easier time integrating their wartime experiences into their new civilian life; however, others experience substantial suffering as they come to terms with various severe experiences of war. In the Jewish community, most people probably know somebody who has served in combat, either in the United States or Israeli militaries, and some may be carrying psychological, emotional, or moral injuries that are not necessarily visible to outsiders' eyes. The more we can help create welcoming, compassionate, and understanding communities, the more support we can provide to those struggling with these invisible wounds.

Cat Got Your Tongue?
Chazal's Tips for
Overcoming Stage Fright (34a)

נֹצֵר פִּיו שֹׁמֵר נַפְשׁוֹ, פֹּשֵׂק שְׂפָתָיו מְחִתָּה לוֹ

He who guards his tongue preserves his life;
He who opens wide his lips, it is his ruin.
— Mishlei 13:3

Warren Buffett, one of the wealthiest and most famous investors in history, described one of his greatest obstacles that he overcame:

> Somebody once said that the chains of habit are too light to be felt until they're too heavy to be broken. I had been terrified of public speaking. I couldn't do it. I'd throw up. And I knew if I didn't cure it then, I'd never cure it. And so I saw an ad in the paper for the Dale Carnegie Course, which worked on developing your ability to speak in public, and I went down there.... If I hadn't had done that my whole life would have been different. So in my office you will not see the degree I got from the University of Nebraska... [or] the Masters degree I got from Columbia University,

but you'll see the little award certificate I got from the Dale Carnegie Course.

As a matter of fact, every week, the instructor would give a pencil to whoever had done the most with what we'd learned the week before. And so in the fourth or fifth week, I proposed to [my future wife's] mother, and she said yes. And so that week, I won the pencil, I also got engaged....[201]

Many people are familiar with this type of experience, as they manage with spikes in a somewhat unique type of anxiety when they have to perform in front of an audience, known as "performance anxiety," or "stage fright." This anxiety may be different than other types of social anxiety[202] which they found can have an effect on performers of a wide range of tasks,[203] such as test-taking,[204] public speaking,[205]

201. Kunhardt, P. W., Kunhardt, T., Kunhardt, G., Chuang, C., Buffett, W., MacWilliams, S. S., Kunhardt Films (Firm), ... Warner Home Video (Firm),. (2017). *Becoming Warren Buffett.*

202. Blöte, A. W., Kint, M. J., Miers, A. C., & Westenberg, P. M. (2009). The relation between public speaking anxiety and social anxiety: A review. *Journal of Anxiety Disorders, 23*(3), 305-313.

203. E.g., Salmon, P. G. (1990). A psychological perspective on musical performance anxiety: A review of the literature. *Medical Problems of Performing Artists, 5*(1), 2-11.

204. E.g., Cassady, J. C., & Johnson, R. E. (2002). Cognitive test anxiety and academic performance. *Contemporary Educational Psychology, 27*(2), 270-295.

205. Bodie, G. D. (2010). A racing heart, rattling knees, and ruminative thoughts: Defining, explaining, and treating public speaking anxiety. *Communication Education, 59*(1), 70-105.

competitive sports,[206] and the performing arts,[207] among other domains of public or evaluative performances.

Over the past fifty-plus years, a great deal of research has been devoted to understanding various types, features, and effects of anxiety, and, as such, a thorough review of how anxiety works is well beyond the scope of this chapter. Nevertheless, some basic principles have emerged from the extensive literature and various theoretical models focusing on anxiety. Although no consensus exists regarding a specific theory for performance anxiety, most models include some basic components. One major feature of the experience of anxiety in general, and performance anxiety in particular, may be referred to as a "cognitive style," which refers to certain tendencies in the way a person thinks or evaluates a situation. Some of these cognitive styles relate to how a person assesses threat in the environment, whether a person catastrophizes the perceived threat, and, especially in the case of performance anxiety, the degree to which a person is sensitive to the perception or reality that the audience's attention is focused directly on him. Not surprisingly, a person whose cognitive style leads to increased focused on the perceived threat and catastrophic outcome may also experience difficulty concentrating or memory lapses, as his cognitive capacity is diminished during these anxious episodes.

A second feature of the experience of performance anxiety includes physiological responses associated with fear and panic,

206. Woodman, T. I. M., & Hardy, L. E. W. (2003). The relative impact of cognitive anxiety and self-confidence upon sport performance: A meta-analysis. *Journal of Sports Sciences, 21*(6), 443-457.
207. Wilson, G. D. (2002). *Psychology for performing artists* (2nd ed.). London, UK: Whurr.

such as increased heart rate, sweating, changes in breathing rhythm, and gastrointestinal distress. A person may also exhibit behavioral effects, such as trembling, tensed muscles, fidgeting hands, facial expressions, or avoidance.[208] These three basic components—the cognitive style, physiological changes, and behavioral effects—are three frequently identified aspects of anxiety, and treatment options typically focus on addressing a combination of these three features of performance anxiety.

The reality that performing in front of others generates anxiety and affects cognitive performance, a robust finding by many social scientists, was also recognized by Chazal, and their understanding of performance anxiety may play a role in *halachah* as well. Below, I will present two examples in *halachah* that demonstrate the recognition of performance anxiety, as well as suggest two techniques for managing performance anxiety that emerge from the halachic discussions, and are consistent with cognitive-behavioral principles in approaching the challenge posed by performance anxiety.

Example 1: The Nervous Kohen

The Mishnah (*Berachos* 34a) rules:

> ...If there is no *kohen* [in *shul*] besides [the *chazzan* to recite the Priestly Blessing], he should not recite the Priestly Blessing [himself].

This Mishnah is set in a time period during which the *chazzan* would recite the prayers by heart. It presents a case in which the *chazzan* is a

_____

208. Salmon (1990) cited above.

kohen, which would require him to recite the priestly blessing during the course of his recitation of the *Amidah*; however, the Mishnah rules that if no other *kohen* is present, the *chazzan* should not recite the blessings. Rashi explains the rationale for this *halachah*:

> Perhaps he will not be able to return [to the proper place in the recitation] beginning with "*sim shalom*," as he will become confused due to *eimas ha-tzibbur* (fear of the congregation).

A simple reading of the Mishnah does not seem to require the addition of these final two words. One might have thought that the cognitive challenge identified by the Mishnah relates to memory retrieval: someone who is accustomed to reciting the *Amidah* straight through would get thrown off by the addition of the *Birkas Kohanim* (priestly blessing) into his recitation. This alternative read would be supported by the ruling of *Shulchan Aruch*[209] that for uncommonly recited *tefillos* one should not recite them from memory and should, instead, either practice beforehand (when he does not have a *siddur* [prayer book]), or, as is our practice, pray using a *siddur*. The concern is that a person who breaks his normal flow in davening with additions or changes for holidays will have a difficult time returning to his regular prayer following the interruption. Anecdotally, I have observed a similar phenomenon nowadays regarding *chazzanim* returning to the Shabbos or Yom Tov tune for *sim shalom*, following a break in the cantorial *nusach* (traditional melody) for the *Birkas Kohanim*; unseasoned *ba'alei tefillah*, who use the traditional tune

---

209. *Orach Chaim* 100:1, see *Mishnah Berurah* there.

until that point, sometimes have difficulty readjusting once they have interrupted the flow. Similarly, *ba'alei tefillah* for *kabbalas Shabbos* who try to switch tunes for the *lo teivoshi* stanza may have trouble recalling the second tune immediately after completing the first one.

Indeed, the Talmud Yerushalmi (*Berachos* 4:4) indicates that even one of the Amoraim had difficulty returning to the flow of his prayers once he got out of rhythm. The Gemara there presents an opinion that in order for *tefillah* not be performed by rote, one should add one's own personal prayers to the traditional text. Rabbi Zeira, however, comments that he does not follow this suggestion, "for whenever I do this [i.e., add my own prayers], I make a mistake [in the text of the required prayers]."[210]

Although this explanation of the Mishnah, that we are concerned about the *chazzan* being able to return to regular *tefillah* as a result of a deficit in memory retrieval, seems plausible and supported by various sources, in this instance Rashi adds the phrase at the end of his commentary, "because of *eimas ha-tzibbur*;" he seems to be describing something akin to stage fright.[211] Using more contemporary psychological language, we might explain the

---

210. The Talmud Bavli (*Berachos* 29b) quotes Rabbi Zeira with a slight difference: "I could introduce a novel element in every prayer, but I am afraid that perhaps I will become confused." In other words, Rabbi Zeira in the Bavli is concerned that he might lose his train of thought, while in the Talmud Yerushalmi he seems to say that it actually happened.

211. Notably, the term *eimas ha-tzibbur* is used in different ways by the commentators in different parts of *Shas*. Nevertheless, in this instance, stage fright seems to be most straightforward way of understanding its usage.

phenomenon as follows. The *chazzan*, who is, among other things, putting on a public performance, experiences worry or anxiety that he may mess up in front of the crowd, and this experience is exacerbated as he senses the direct focus of the congregation on himself. As a result of this anxiety, the *chazzan* then experiences restricted cognitive capacity to shift focus to the continuation of the recitation as he attempts to redirect his memory to the next blessing of the *Amidah*. The concern according to Rashi is not related to memory issues per se; instead, Rashi's explanation focuses on the way that performance anxiety impacts one's ability to retrieve information.

Based on this view of Rashi's position, the following ruling of the Mishnah should also be interpreted differently than what it might appear at first glance. The Mishnah states that if someone is sufficiently self-assured to be able to return to the recitation of the *Amidah*, he may recite the priestly blessings as well. In its simplest terms, the Mishnah is adding a law based on principles of memory retrieval: if a person is confident that he will be able to get back on track, there is no problem interrupting his flow to recite the *Birkas Kohanim*. However, according to Rashi, this law is actually based on principles of managing with the anxiety induced by performing in front of the congregation, as he writes:

> [This ruling] is to say that if he is confident that his mind will not become confused due to *eimas ha-tzibbur*.

Once again, Rashi adds the two final words that, on their face, are unnecessary according to the first, simpler interpretation of the

Mishnah. But according to Rashi's approach, the extra words are consistent with first clause of the Mishnah, framing the issue around the question of how performance anxiety can affect one's cognitive functioning, and how a person might manage the deleterious effects.

Although it is clearly not the direct point of the Mishnah, the second ruling implies that effective interventions may be possible to aid with performance anxiety, an idea consistent with a cognitive model of anxiety. Generally speaking, challenges with anxiety include two layers: first, a person feels anxiety about performing; the second layer involves worry about the worry, such that a person may worry that his performance will be negatively affected as a result of the anxiety that he will feel when he's performing. Interventions based on a cognitive model aim to reduce either or both levels of anxiety, thus freeing a person to perform at the level of his training.

With that in mind, let us consider the intervention suggested by our Mishnah and the *halachah* that emerges from it. According to later *poskim*, one fulfills the Mishnah's condition of being "self-assured" if he uses a *siddur* while praying and leading services.[212] From a psychological perspective, this technique may provide certain cognitive benefits aiding with the experience of performance of anxiety. Using a printed *siddur* likely leads to perceived, and actual, mastery over the text he is reciting. This sense of mastery is an important aspect to an intervention for performance anxiety. First, if he does experience anxiety while leading services, the cognitive load necessary to simply read from the *siddur* is far less than that required to recall from memory the text he is meant to recite. Second, this sense of mastery would also likely reduce his level of anxiety about

---

212. *Mishnah Berurah* 128:76.

feeling anxiety, because he knows he has the tools necessary to keep himself on track.

Example 2: Starting Young

A second example that provides insight into possible interventions for performance anxiety emerges from a *teshuvah* of Rav Ovadia Yosef regarding boys under the age of *bar mitzvah* receiving an *aliyah* and reading from the Torah for the congregation. He writes that, in accordance with various Acharonim, the prevailing custom in Yerushalayim is to give minors *aliyos* on Shabbos, and adds the following:

> This is especially the case when the boy's voice is pleasant, and he is able to read the Torah expertly with the correct *trop*. And this is in order to teach and train him that when he becomes a *bar mitzvah* he will be able to serve as a *shaliach tzibbur* [prayer leader] to fulfil the obligation of the congregation and *will not be too anxious due to the eimas ha-tzibbur.*[213]

In this last line, Rav Ovadia Yosef provides several insights into preventing and managing performance anxiety. The first is the recognition that younger kids, on average, are less prone to experience performance anxiety than are adults. This assumption seems to be supported by research spanning forty years, that social anxiety, a similar phenomenon to performance anxiety, has an average age of

---

213. *Yechaveh Da'as* 4:23.

onset around or after the time of *bar mitzvah*.[214] A second insight is that habituating youth to performing, which includes dealing with whatever level of performance anxiety that may arise, can help kids be more comfortable performing as they get older. In psychological terms, this might be referred to as improving a child's sense of self-efficacy, which refers to one's belief that he is able to exercise control over difficult or threatening things in the environment.[215] Giving a child the opportunity to develop strong self-efficacy prior to *bar mitzvah* age can be a powerful tool in preventing the development of debilitating performance anxiety in the future.

Lesson for Today

While almost everybody experiences some level of anxiety prior to performing, persistent, debilitating performance anxiety affects a relatively small percentage of the general population. For people in the latter group, even experts in the field acknowledge that there is no single technique that is effective for everyone for treating or managing performance anxiety.[216] A range of strategies has been

---

214. E.g., Marks, I. M., & Gelder, M. G. (1966). Different ages of onset in varieties of phobia. *American Journal of Psychiatry,* 123(2), 218-221; Kessler, R. C., Berglund, P., Demler, O., Jin, R., Merikangas, K. R., & Walters, E. E. (2005). Lifetime prevalence and age-of-onset distributions of DSM-IV disorders in the National Comorbidity Survey Replication. *Archives of General Psychiatry,* 62(6), 593-602.

215. E.g., Bandura, A. (1988). Self-efficacy conception of anxiety. *Anxiety research,* 1(2), 77-98.

216. Lazarus, A. A., & Abramovitz, A. (2004). A multimodal behavioral approach to performance anxiety. *Journal of Clinical Psychology,* 60(8), 831-840.

offered by scientists, clinicians, and those who have overcome such fears themselves, and those who experience substantial impairment due to their anxiety should consider consulting with professionals trained in treating anxiety, or at least investigate suggestions by those who have overcome the challenge.

It is also worth considering what we may be able to gain from the insights of Chazal and the halachic sources regarding our stance toward performance anxiety in ourselves and others. As I have come to see through my clinical experience, many people take a judgmental stance toward anxiety, thinking that they should not have it, that it is bad, that it represents an unacceptable flaw or weakness. This self-critical judgment itself can, at times, become an additional barrier to managing or overcoming their stage-fright. But the stance emerging from the Talmudic sources above reveal a dramatically different, present-focused, non-judgmental stance that can be helpful in reducing the impairment a person faces from the experience of performance anxiety. The *chazzan* is not condemned for having anxiety that may disturb his prayer; instead, the Mishnah accepts as a reality that some people, despite their best intentions, will experience anxiety. This approach of non-judgmental acceptance, and the recognition that this experience has been shared by others for thousands of years, can be helpful to reframe the frustrations of performance anxiety and provide some element of relief.

A second consideration that emerges from this Mishnah relates to accommodating others' anxiety. We can imagine what might happen if Chazal had not given this instruction—the *kohen* with performance anxiety would avoid being *chazzan* altogether, so as to avoid a scenario that he is embarrassed for losing his place. By

213

adjusting the *halachah* to account for the anxious *kohen*, we are also, incidentally, setting him up for success as a *shaliach tzibbur*, which benefits both the *kohen* and congregation. Following Chazal's example, we might ask ourselves how we can accommodate and encourage the success of those in our communities who experience anxiety or other circumstances that make full participation in communal life difficult.

Just as with other forms of anxiety, managing performance anxiety can be complicated, as there is no single template for how to treat it. Nevertheless, from these insights into performance anxiety that emerge from *halachah*, we can learn important skills for reducing the anxiety or its impact. As a community as well, we can learn from the accommodating and non-judgmental attitude of Chazal how to be more sensitive and understanding toward our own and others' anxiety.

Do You Understand the
Words Coming Out of My Mouth?
Halachic Implications of
Accents and Language Processing (35a)

וּבְרָא ה' אֱלֹקִים יָת אָדָם עַפְרָא מִן אַדְמְתָא
וּנְפַח בְּאַפּוֹהִי נִשְׁמְתָא דְחַיֵּי וַהֲוַת בְּאָדָם רוּחַ מְמַלְלָא:

And the Lord God created man, dirt from the
ground, and He blew into his nostrils a living soul,
and it was for a speaking spirit in man.
— Targum Onkelos Bereishis 2:7

Even though he was born and raised in South Carolina, Stephen Colbert, a late-night talk show host who started his television career as a satirical news anchor, speaks with what is often called a "General American" accent. This accent, which is considered to not have any regional markers that would allow a listener to identify the native region of the speaker, has long been identified as a preferred accent for those who interact with the public, from news-people to telemarketers.[217] When asked how he has such an accent, despite his southern background, Colbert replied:

217. Retrieved from: https://www.nytimes.com/1991/07/21/realestate/focus-omaha-s-becoming-the-emerald-city-of-the-plains.html?searchResultPosition=5.

At a very young age, I decided I was not gonna have a Southern accent. Because people, when I was a kid watching TV, if you wanted to use a shorthand that someone was stupid, you gave the character a Southern accent. And that's not true. Southern people are not stupid. But I didn't wanna seem stupid. I wanted to seem smart. And so I thought, "Well, you can't tell where newsmen are from."

As Colbert recognized, accents and dialects represent more than just patterns in how people make sounds of words. Accents can identify a person's place of origin, affect how people perceive various qualities in the speaker, and, as I will describe below, affect how language itself is processed by the speaker and by the listener.

Language processing, which refers to the way people use words to communicate with others, and how these communications are understood by the listener, is among the most complex areas of study in psychology. The way accents relate to language processing, then, is similarly complex. As such, the ideas presented in this chapter are not discussed in the context of the diverse theoretical approaches to various aspects of language processing; instead, they are meant to give a few examples regarding into how accents and language processing play a role in Torah and *halachah*, and how our appreciation of both the Torah and contemporary scientific sources regarding accents and language processing may provide deeper insight into each of them.

Regional Accents

The scientific study of foreign and regional accents, and how accented language is processed, has received a great deal of attention in recent years as voice-activated artificial intelligence (AI) has become increasingly ubiquitous. One common challenge, however, is that people with diverse accents show great phonetic variety in producing identical words, which creates challenges for developing technology for AI's understanding of natural language. As reported by the *Washington Post*,[218] Amazon Echo and Google Home, two of the most common home-based voice-activated AI devices, both perform with varying levels of accuracy depending on the speaker's accent.

The presence of regional accents, while generating new problems as new technologies emerge, was recognized thousands of years ago, particularly regarding the pronunciation of consonants. Perhaps the most famous story in Torah literature related to accents is found in the story of the civil war between Yiftach's army from Gil'ad and the people of Ephraim (*Shoftim* Chapter 12):

> Gil'ad occupied the crossings of the Jordan against Ephraim, so it was that when the "rabble of Ephraim" would say, "Let me cross," the men of Gil'ad would say to him, "Are you an Ephrathite?" and he would answer, "No." Then they would say to him, "Now say, '*Shibboles*,'" but he said, "*Sibboles*"— for he could not enunciate properly. Then they would seize him and slaughter him by the crossings of the Jordan.

In this instance, a regional accent—the pronunciation of an "sh" sounds as an "s" sound—was used as a marker to identify people

---

218. Retrieved from https://www.washingtonpost.com/graphics/2018/business/alexa-does-not-understand-your-accent/?utm_term=.74ca08443379.

from Ephraim, which led to their subsequent death. An obvious question arises regarding why the people of Ephraim would not try to shift their accent. Radak and others imply that the problem was not simply that this sound was *difficult* for them to pronounce; rather, it seems that they were *unable* to make the "sh" sound properly.[219] In fact, as researchers have found that those with alternate speech patterns may not perceive the differences between various consonant sounds,[220] it is possible that those from Ephraim did not even notice that they were saying the words differently. It is likely that some people from Ephraim successfully adjusted their speech and were able to pass, as studies have shown that it is possible for adults to learn how to make new sounds[221]; nevertheless, it is clear that this is not a skill that can be picked up easily by most people.

---

219. Another possible answer is that they did not know they would be receiving this test for passage, and it was kept secret by the people of Gil'ad until the end of the war. According to this approach, had they been aware, they may have been able to change their pronunciation of the consonant. This second answer is supported by the commentator's suggestion that *shibboles* refers to the flow of water, and the people asking to cross would have asked, naively, for the ability to cross the river, *"shibboles ha-nahar ha-zeh a'avor"* (Rashi).

220. E.g., Guion, S. G., Flege, J. E., Akahane-Yamada, R., & Pruitt, J. C. (2000). An investigation of current models of second language speech perception: The case of Japanese adults' perception of English consonants. *The Journal of the Acoustical Society of America, 107*(5), 2711-2724.

221. For several citations, see: Flege, J. E., Takagi, N., & Mann, V. (1995). Japanese adults can learn to produce English/I/and/l/ accurately. *Language and Speech, 38*(1), 25-55.

In modern times, the outcome of pronouncing consonants differently is unlikely to be so severe; however, there are some potential social consequences that accents generate that present challenges to those who possess these accents. As some research has found, people quickly assign social categories to others based on their accents,[222] which, as a result, may lead to the listener assuming a host of stereotypes about the speaker. More broadly, this idea is known as "social salience," which is the concept that the form of spoken language evokes social meaning.[223] In the general world, some examples include replacing the "th" sound with an "f" sound, known as th-fronting (e.g., "I frew the ball" instead of "I threw the ball")—this variation is typically seen as reflecting a lower socioeconomic status for different groups in the United Kingdom and the United States. Just as Colbert wanted to avoid the stigma being grouped with southern American stereotypes, people with other accents that are considered "lower-class" may also experience a sense of stigma by virtue of the way they speak.

The reality that accents are associated with social categories can also be seen in the Jewish community, particularly among those who want to fit into a new social group than the one in which they grew up. For example, for modern Orthodox students who want to become part of a yeshivish community, long "o" sounds become "ai" or "oi" sounds, "r" sounds become more guttural, and there may be a

222. Pietraszewski, D., & Schwartz, A. (2014). Evidence that accent is a dimension of social categorization, not a byproduct of perceptual salience, familiarity, or ease-of-processing. *Evolution and Human Behavior*, 35(1), 43-50.

223. Labov, William. 2001. *Principles of linguistic change: Social factors.* Oxford: Blackwell.

tendency to accent the first syllable in a word instead of the last (such as "TOI-rah" instead of "To-RAH"). Alternatively, Americans who make Aliyah to *tzioni* communities in Israel will change a number of vowel sounds, such as the *kamatz, cholam,* or *tzeireh* to sound more Israeli, and change the "r" to a rolling sound. To the trained ear, most newcomers to communities retain some of their previous accent features; nevertheless, the intentional changes to their accent is meant to help integrate them into a specific social community to which they wish to become a part.

Phonologically Similar Letters

A second aspect of language processing that has relevance to Talmudic and halachic sources relates to the phonological similarities (i.e., letters that sound similar to one another) between different letters in Hebrew. Chazal have identified a number of phonologically similar letters that speakers, for thousands of years, have had difficulty differentiating between verbally, namely *hei, ches,* and *ayin* (and some texts including *aleph*). This trend was identified as early as prior to the destruction of the Second Temple regarding two Tannaim, Shmaya and Avtalion. The Mishnah in *Eiduyos* (1:3) records a ruling of Hillel, which he received from his teachers, Shmaya and Avtalion, with two curious words:

Hillel says: "A full *hin* [*melo hin*] of drawn water [*mayim sha'uvim*] invalidates a *mikveh.*

The term *melo hin* is odd for two reasons. First, the term *hin* was used in the Torah describe a certain volume, but was not the typical word used in the time of the Rabbis; the commentators explain that in this instance, there was a preference to use the Biblical word. The second odd word choice is *melo,* which does not seem to add anything to the meaning of the ruling. Regarding this question, Rambam on the Mishnah explains that as converts, Shmaya and Avtalion's accent was such that the word *hin* was not distinguishable to the word *ein,* which means "not." As such, listeners might interpret the ruling that drawn water *does not* invalidate a *mikveh*—literally the opposite of the intended ruling[224]; for this reason, they added the word *melo* to indicate that they were referring to a volume. Rav Ovadia Bartenura, who lived in the 15th century, adds that this is "just as people nowadays are unable to properly pronounce these letters."

Although this difficulty to verbally differentiate between these letters might be considered a quirk of accents that develop as people from various cultures interface with Hebrew, Chazal seem to view the phonological similarities between these letters as intrinsic features of the language. Take, for example, this passage found in the Talmud Yerushalmi (*Shabbos* 7:2):

> There are 39 primary categories of *melachah* on Shabbos. From where in the Torah do we see that there are 39 categories?...Rabbi Yosi ben Chanina said... the Torah writes "These are the things" [*eileh ha-devarim*—*eileh* is spelled ‏א.ל.ה‎; *Shemos* 35:1) ...[based on the numerical values of the letters] *aleph* = 1; *lamed* = 30; *hei* = 5; *davar* is 1; *devarim* (plural) is 2; which altogether equal 39.

---

224. This fear that listeners would misinterpret a ruling based on phonetically similar words is not unfounded. For example, see *Pesachim* 42a regarding the story of Rav Matna.

The Sages from Caesarea say [you can learn it all from the word *eileh*]: *aleph* = 1; *lamed* = 30; *ches* = 8; which altogether equal 39, as the Rabbis do not differentiate between *hei* and *ches* when making *drashos*.

Apparently, letters that are phonetically similar can be interchangeable when there is a meaningful *drasha* to be made with the alternate letter, even, as Rav Bartenura explained, the similarities are at least in part due to accents that can be affected by many factors. In addition to the *hei/ches* switches mentioned above, the Gemara also uses the *shin/samech* phonetic similarity, the one found in *Sefer Shoftim*, to make *drashos*.[225]

All of the *drashos* mentioned above are of the aggadic type, which, in some ways, makes the use of accents less surprising, as they do not impact practical *halahcah* in meaningful ways. After all, one might argue that the verse should be considered an *asmachta b'alma* (supporting text, but not the source for a *halacha*), and the moral lesson being taught by Chazal would stand independently of the quirky accents that lead to phonetic similarities between dissimilar letters. The following *drasha* (*Berachos* 35a) however, is halachic in nature, indicating that the use of phonetic similarities, even those that may be due to accented speech, should be seen as fundamental to the language. The Mishnah details the appropriate blessings for

---

225. E.g., *Sanhedrin* 70a that makes use of both the *shin/samech* and *hei/ches* switches; *Sotah* 3a; Talmud Yerushalmi, *Berachos* 2:4 (see *Sha'ar Shimon* ad loc. who argues that the Talmud Yerushalmi is not referring to the *shin/samech* switch).

fruit, and the Gemara cites a verse regarding fruit of the fourth year as the source, as the verse says, "...all its fruit should be sanctified to laud [*hillulim*, in plural] Hashem." The Gemara then asks:

And did this verse: "Sanctified to laud" come for that purpose? This verse is necessary to derive other matters. One being that the Merciful One said: Redeem it [from the word *chillul*, "de-sanctify, redeem," which sounds like *hillul*] and then eat it.

According to this *drasha*, the interchangeability of the *hei* and *ches* cannot be regarded simply as an accident of accents.[226] Rather, even if we accept Rav Bartenura's comment that it is due to people's inability to properly pronounce the letters, the resulting phonetic similarity is intrinsic to the understanding of the words.

Phonological Similarity and Semantic Priming

It is also worth considering an additional phenomenon, recognized by Chazal, that phonological similarity of one word to another can affect how we process and understand the word, even if the spoken word was based on mistaken or accented pronunciation. Perhaps the best example of this is reflected in one of the most famous instances of caution against mispronouncing a word. Tosafos (*Berachos* 15b), based on the Talmud Yerushalmi, instructs that when reciting *keriyas*

---

226. Notably, Ra'avad cited in Ritva argues that the *drasha* is not based on the interchangeability of these letters, but his approach seems to be rejected by Ritva.

Shema, one should emphasize the "z" sound in the phrase *lema'an tizkeru,* "so that you will remember," so that it does not sound like *tiskeru,* "you will be rewarded," which would improperly imply that we perform the commandments on the condition of receiving a reward.[227] At first glance, this instruction seems odd—after all, Tosafos is not arguing that a person may come to mistakenly believe that the word is truly *tiskeru.* Instead, Tosafos seems to be arguing that even though a person is fully aware that the correct word is *tizkeru,* he will begin to think about the meaning and implication of the *tiskeru* should he be lax in the correct pronunciation.

The psychological foundation of this *halachah* seems to be the concept of "priming," which refers to a cognitive process in which one word, sound, idea, or item makes our brains more sensitive to a second word, sound, idea, or item that our brain perceives as being similar. For an example of how priming relates to accented or differently pronounced speech, a recent study compared Americans with New York accents to Americans with a more generic type of American accent.[228] They examined whether the sound "slenda" would prime the word "thin." What they found is that for New Yorkers, for whom dropping the "r" in "slender" is a typical aspect of their regional accent, the word "thin" was primed; however, for non-New Yorkers, "slenda" did not prime the word "thin." In other

---

227. Commentators cite other examples within *keriyas Shema* for which mispronunciations can lead to dramatically different meaning; however, this example is probably the most commonly stressed by the general public.

228. Sumner, M., & Samuel, A. G. (2009). The effect of experience on the perception and representation of dialect variants. *Journal of Memory and Language, 60*(4), 487-501.

words, for New Yorkers, a regionally-specific accent brought to mind an associated idea, namely slender-thin, through the process of semantic priming.

This process, or one more specifically referred to as "semantic priming,"[229] may also be the driver behind the *halachah* cited by Tosafos. When a person hears the word *tiskeru*, even if it is the incorrect pronunciation, the brain processes the word as it is spoken; as a result, the brain is "primed" to consider ideas of being rewarded for the performance of *mitzvos*.

Lesson for Today

As the *Chafetz Chaim* and many other scholars describe, there are many *mitzvos*, both positive and negative, that involve speech and language, such as *tefillah* and *keriyas Shema*, kiddush, Torah study and teaching, comforting mourners, avoiding *lashon hara* (gossip), and many others. The abundance of *mitzvos* and regulations surrounding speech is not surprising, as, according to many commentators, it is this ability to generate language that reflects our Divine image.[230]

On a personal level, it is worth considering how we relate to others' way of speaking. Sometimes, if our first time encountering someone is on the phone, the first thing that we know about another person is how he sounds. What judgments are we making about the person just based on his voice and how he pronounces words?

---

229. Rastle, K., & Brysbaert, M. (2006). Masked phonological priming effects in English: Are they real? Do they matter?. *Cognitive Psychology, 53*(2), 97-145; Rogers, C. S. (2017). Semantic priming, not repetition priming, is to blame for false hearing. *Psychonomic Bulletin & Review, 24*(4), 1194-1204.
230. See Onkelos, *Bereishis* 2:7.

Are those judgments fair? Just as Mr. Colbert noticed, do we think less of others because they sound or say words a certain way? The research presented above suggests that although these judgments may be somewhat automatic, they also may not be correct or helpful. The more we can refrain from, delay, or challenge these judgments about others, particularly regarding the snap judgments based on superficial qualities, the better our relationships and interactions with others will be.

Don't Tread on Me

Microaggressions in Talmudic
and Halachic Literature (58b)

לֹעֵג לָרָשׁ חֵרֵף עֹשֵׂהוּ שָׂמֵחַ לְאֵיד לֹא יִנָּקֶה

One who mocks a pauper insults his Maker;
one who rejoices in another's misfortune will not be exonerated.
— Mishlei 17:5

In November 2013, Dr. Val Rust's classroom in UCLA was the
center of a protest effort that was covered nationwide. According
to reports,[231] following the controversial protests Dr. Rust, a
professor with decades of experience in UCLA, was presented
with an ultimatum: agree to remain off-campus for the remainder
of the semester, or the school would pursue disciplinary actions
against him. What was the basis of the protest against the 79-year
old professor? According to the protesters, Dr. Rust was guilty of
perpetrating "racial microaggressions" against students of color.
While many students and faculty in the university and around the
country denounced the protesters and supported Dr. Rust and his

231. https://www.city-journal.org/html/microaggression-
farce-13679.html.

reputation, how are we to understand the great impact of these perceived microaggressions that sparked such passionate protests?

What Are Microaggressions?

The term "microaggression," though not new,[232] has gained greater importance in recent years. Indeed, some psychologists have traced the theoretical elements to Freud's 1901 work, *The Pathology of Everyday Life.*[233] Nevertheless, the focused academic study of microaggressions took off following the seminal article by Sue, in which they provide a detailed picture of the role of microaggressions in society generally, and psychology in particular.[234]

Sue defines the term racial microaggression as "brief and commonplace daily verbal, behavioral, and environmental indignities, whether intentional or unintentional, that communicate hostile, derogatory, or negative racial slights and insults to the target person or group," although the word "racial" could surely be replaced by other aspects of identity. For anyone who ever felt vulnerable, he can appreciate the sensitivity to these "brief and commonplace" occurrences, despite their inconspicuous nature.

---

232. It seems that the term was coined in the late 1970s in the following article: Pierce, C., Carew, J., Pierce-Gonzalez, D., & Willis, D. (1978). An experiment in racism: TV commercials. In C. Pierce (Ed.), *Television and Education* (pp. 62–88). Beverly Hills, CA: Sage.

233. Schacht, T. E. (2008). A broader view of racial microaggression in psychotherapy. *American Psychologist, 63*(4), 273.

234. Sue, D. W., Capodilupo, C. M., Torino, G. C., Bucceri, J. M., Holder, A., Nadal, K. L., & Esquilin, M. (2007). Racial microaggressions in everyday life: Implications for clinical practice. *American Psychologist, 62*(4), 271.

For the observant Jew in the contemporary world, examples of possible microaggressions are plentiful: comments about leaving early on Fridays or Jewish holidays, or bosses who provide pushback; limited access to kosher food; comments in the media about Jewish stereotypes; disregard of anti-Semitism; etc. Jews may also be the aggressors, as attitudes and comments about Jews of differing observance levels, gentiles, or other "outsider" groups may reflect disparaging, offensive opinions.

A common facet of these microaggressions, as opposed to macroaggressions, is that the aggressors, for the most part, are able to claim they meant no harm, and may even argue that they were being sensitive to cultural differences. And perhaps, as the definition notes, the harm is entirely unintentional. Indeed, who can really know what is in a person's heart: hostility or honor, antagonism or admiration. But the injured party, who in that moment is vulnerable, can tell that they are being put down, ever so slightly, and are unable to defend themselves from a subtle attack at their identity.

Talmudic Examples of Microaggressions

Before discussing the overlap between the language and sensitivities of contemporary researchers and the Talmudic Sages, a few points are necessary. First, contemporary research and activism has largely (though not exclusively) focused on racial microaggressions; however, in this chapter, I will focus on the general principle of microaggressions. Second, the intentional, plainly measurable types of aggressions, verbal and otherwise, are not my focus here. Countless pages of Rabbinic literature have detailed the gravity of shaming others publicly and purposefully. Instead, I focus on the less perceptible types of aggressions found in classical Jewish texts, including those that are intentional yet subtle, as well as those that are unintentional. It is important to note that not all contemporary researchers agree with the characterization, presence, or impact of microaggressions,[235] as research into various aspects of microaggressions is in its relative infancy.

One remarkable parallel sets the stage for understanding the degree of overlap between Chazal and contemporary thinkers. While overlapping concepts between the two is both expected and not unique, in many cases the language used to describe comparable principles is often very different, as would be expected with the cultural and chronological gap. However, in the case of microaggressions, the language used by the Sages is nearly identical to that used by modern researchers, as shown in the following example. The passage in *Shemos* 22:20-23 warns against afflicting the vulnerable, and cautions: "If you afflict them in any way (using the same root for afflict twice,"ענה תענה"), for if they cry out at all to Me, I will surely hear their cry." The Midrash notes the unusual use of the repeated word for "afflict": [This] refers to both major afflictions and minor afflictions (*innuy merubah* and *innuy mu'at*)[236]—or, in contemporary terms, macroaggressions and microaggressions. For those who offend the vulnerable in either way, Hashem testifies that "My wrath shall blaze, and I shall kill you by the sword, and your wives will be widows and your children orphans," measure for measure.

---

235. E.g., Lilienfeld, S. O. (2017). Microaggressions: Strong claims, inadequate evidence. *Perspectives on Psychological Science, 12*(1), 138-169.

236. *Mechilta*, ad loc. See also *Torah Sheleimah, Shemos* 22:22 note 378.

If the stakes are so high, it is instructive to consider what the Sages considered to be a microaggression. The Midrash continues regarding two of the great martyrs of Jewish history:[237]

When Rabbi Yishmael and Rabbi Shimon were taken to be executed, Rabbi Shimon said to Rabbi Yishmael: "Master, my heart is faint because I do not know for what reason I am being killed." Rabbi Yishmael responded to Rabbi Shimon, "Did it ever happen that a person came to you for a judgement or with a question, and you delayed him until you finished your drink, or you tied you sandal, or you put on your cloak? And the Torah says, 'if you afflict them at all,' referring to both a large affliction and a small affliction." [On hearing this, Rabbi Shimon] replied: "Master, you have comforted me."[238]

---

237. Notably, an alternate version of this story is quoted in *Mishnah Berurah* 53:35.

238. One may wonder if the reason that Rabbi Yishmael does not seem to be bothered by the same question about himself is related to the topic at hand. Did he already complete a self-reflection and determine that he, too, was guilty of these acts? Did he not question the Divine decree to being with? Was there another occurrence in his life that he considered more relevant? A close read of the Midrash may highlight this principle in a more profound way. After all, why wouldn't Rabbi Shimon ask Rabbi Yishmael about why both of them are being executed? Perhaps Rabbi Shimon, even in his moment of despair, had the presence of mind not to ask a question that assumes Rabbi Yishmael would engage in an act so egregious as to warrant death. The Midrash is teaching that even such a person as Rabbi Shimon, who is so cautious even during these overwhelming times, may have committed these microaggressions for which he is held responsible.

A close read of this passage demonstrates a critical point. First, though the verses specify widows, orphans, and converts, Rabbi Yishmael assumes the same principles apply to anyone who is in a vulnerable position. Second, Rabbi Yishmael chooses examples of when the slights Rabbi Shimon might have committed were by way of his position of authority, as Rabbi Shimon tended to personal needs rather than the urgent needs of the petitioner.[239] Rabbi Yishmael seems to be arguing that by tending to his own personal, non-urgent needs in the face of an anxious vulnerable party, he is using his perch of power in a way that afflicts another person—this slight of the vulnerable person brings about the full wrath of the verse's punishment. Obviously, Rabbi Shimon never intended for those actions to be hurtful, but he ultimately recognizes the harm they caused nonetheless.

The level of scrutiny of Rabbi Shimon's actions would be impossible for most of us withstand. Still, the rest of us are not absolved from being cautious about slighting others in small ways, as demonstrated by a Talmudic passage (*Berachos* 6b). There, the Gemara asserts, based on a verse in *Yeshayahu* that refers to "theft from the poor," that a person who is greeted by his friend and does not return the greeting is considered a robber. Rashi comments on this passage:

---

239. In addition to these comments, it is important to consider that Rabbi Yishmael does not argue that the punishment could be warranted if Rabbi Shimon had caused anguish to a vulnerable person by ruling against him according to the law—presumably Rabbi Shimon would not be responsible for this type of anguish, as he is ruling justly.

Of course, theft from a wealthy person is also [prohibited] as theft! Rather, theft from the poor is specified because [the pauper] has nothing else to steal except for not returning a greeting to him.

In other words, ignoring another person, acting as if he does not deserve even a moment of your attention or time, is an act of stealing his dignity. Though he has suffered no monetary harm, his stature as a human being is the last remaining element of his earthly belongings, and for a moment he has been robbed of even that.

Although this level of sensitivity may seem impossible to obtain, Chazal record that there were people who were this careful about another's dignity. In the course of a discussion regarding the appropriate blessings to make upon seeing parts of the Land of Israel either inhabited or desolate, the Gemara records the following story (*Berachos* 58b):

Ulla and Rav Chisda were once walking along the road when they came upon the doorway of the house of Rav Chana bar Chanilai. Rav Chisda groaned and sighed. Ulla asked him: why are you sighing? Didn't Rav say sighing breaks half of one's body... and Rabbi Yochanan said it even breaks one's whole body?

Rav Chisda replied: How can I not sigh? This house where there were sixty cooks during the day and sixty cooks at night who would cook for anyone in need, and Rav Chana never removed his hand from his pocket because he thought perhaps a well-born poor person may come and in the time that passed for him to put his hand in his pocket [to retrieve a coin] the poor person would be embarrassed.... And they would scatter wheat and barley outside during years of drought so that anyone who was embarrassed to take the grain during the day could come and take it at night. Now that this house has fallen in ruins, how can I not sigh?

Rav Chisda, in his description of Rav Chana's home, is not simply describing the great amount of charity that he performed. He is focusing on the great emotional sensitivity shown to those in vulnerable positions asking for *tzedakah*; Rav Chana recognized the emotional pain that could be present even in the few seconds waiting for him to retrieve a coin from his pocket, so he would keep his hand at the ready to provide the money to the beggar.

Self-Identities in Microaggression

One of the features of microaggressions is that the target feels as though part of his identity is being attacked or belittled. For example, when an African-American receives poor service, he may not attribute that to the restaurant's lousy waitstaff; instead, he may perceive that it is specifically because he is black that the waiter ignores his table. When the boss does not ask for a female employee's opinion, she may not assume this is because the boss is a poor manager; instead, she may conclude that it is because she is a woman that he does not seek out her perspective. In other words, microaggressions occur when the offended party self-identifies as part of a certain group, and perceives that if he were not part of that group he would be treated differently. A Midrash provides a profound insight into this process of self-identity, and how it affects the perception of a microaggression. The verse in *Shemos* (18:9) records that Yisro, Moshe's father-in-law, rejoiced upon hearing Moshe recount all the miracles God performed for the Israelites when He saved them from the Egyptian slavery. The verse uses a very unusual word, *va-yichad*, to describe the joy, prompting the Midrash to add layers of explanation:

> Yisro's skin became prickly (from the root *"chidudin chidudin"*) [because] he was very distressed regarding the destruction of the Egyptians. This is [the source of] the popular saying: Do not disgrace a gentile [lit., "Aramean"] in the presence of a convert, [even] up to the tenth generation [after the conversion].[240]

Obviously, Moshe was not intending to cause distress to his father-in-law while recounting the many miracles performed for the Israelites, and, as noted above, the basic explanation is that Yisro responded very positively to learning about God's miraculous intervention on behalf of the Jewish people. Nevertheless, the Midrash observes that on some level Yisro, a new convert, saw this as a slight against him.

The obligation to show sensitivity to converts is important, but we do not require the Midrash to learn this lesson; indeed, there are explicit verses in the Torah requiring us to be especially cautious against causing harm to converts. A close read reveals that this Midrash is teaching a deeper, more nuanced psychological insight.

---

240. *Sanhedrin* 94a, cited by Rashi, *Shemos* 18:9. See also *Torah Sheleimah*, ad loc. note 54 for some variant texts of the Midrash.

Moshe was describing the ways that the Egyptians were punished by Hashem's miracles—but Yisro was not Egyptian! Why would Yisro be distressed about learning of the Egyptian downfall? The Midrash is demonstrating that in some way, as a stranger to the Jewish people, he felt some affinity for the Egyptians. He was, as converts often are, in a somewhat vulnerable position: without a tribe, not knowing the local customs, and having a foreign accent or not knowing the language well at all. In some ways, Yisro identified with the Egyptians and their pain. In contemporary times, we can observe this reality playing out in many communities. Members of one vulnerable population may identify with the plight of those in other vulnerable populations, and when the powerful group insults the dignity of one group, those in the other group may feel similarly marginalized.

Defending from Microaggressions

The discussions above centered on the elevated sensitivity to others that is required, as a microaggression can be perpetrated unintentionally and with the best intentions. However, in many cases, the speaker may actually intend to offend another person in a subtle way. A second facet of microaggressions that make them particularly challenging to address is that due to their subtlety, the victim cannot defend himself, as the perpetrator can easily deny their ill-intent. This exact point, that people can verbally afflict others in ways that an observer could not determine is full of malice, is the focus of the Talmud's discussion of *ona'as devarim*, loosely defined as verbal oppression (*Bava Metzia* 58b):

If a man is a penitent, one must not say to him, "Remember your former deeds." If he is the son of proselytes he must not be taunted with, "Remember the deeds of your ancestors." If he is a proselyte and comes to study the Torah, one must not say to him, "Shall the mouth that ate unclean and forbidden food, abominable and creeping things, come to study the Torah which was uttered by the mouth of Omnipotence!" If he is visited by suffering, afflicted with disease, or has buried his children, one must not speak to him as his companions spoke to *Iyov* (4:6-7), "is not your fear [of God] your confidence, and your hope the integrity of your ways? Remember, I pray of you, whoever perished, being innocent?"

At first glance, the examples cited by the Gemara seem odd; after all, if the prohibition of *ona'as devarim* is about not afflicting others verbally with malice, as explained by a number of commentators,[241] there seem to be better, more direct examples—the Mishnah could have stated that one must not insult or disparage others. With the examples offered, in addition to the malice behind that words, Chazal are pointing to a nuanced feature of *ona'as devarim*. As Rashi points out,[242] for each of these examples the aggressor can argue "who can tell whether I had evil intentions?" After all, these statements could be seen as inspirational—"See how far you've come!" It is specifically because the perpetrator makes use of this subtle deception, and the target is powerless to defend himself against the offensive statement,

---

241. Rambam, Rav Ovadia Bartenura, ad loc.
242. In his commentary on *Vayikra* 25:17.

that these comments are regarded as *ona'as devarim*. For this reason, the verse concludes "and you should fear your God, for I am the Lord, your God." Though these slights may be indeterminable by other people, God Himself will judge the degree of malice present in the statements.[243]

Lesson for Today

The topic of microaggressions often generates substantial debate. On the one hand, any reasonable person would agree that to whatever extent possible, we should avoid saying things that are hurtful to other. On the other hand, many people find the concept of microaggressions troubling for two primary reasons: first, censoring speech that is innocuous on its surface, but a small group are particularly sensitive to, leads to an unreasonable burden on anyone sharing an opinion that he might offend someone, leading to a decline in open communication; and second, life involves difficulties, and people should be expected to learn how to deal with small offenses. Indeed, as was the case with Dr. Val Rust, it was his job to fairly critique the writing of his students, even if they found his edits offensive.

Though in my view the latter argument has substantial merit, both psychologically and religiously, it is clear that Chazal also

---

243. The Talmudic passage also gives a hint as to the severity these verbal microaggressions, as they are considered even worse than monetary harm in some respects: Rabbi Eleazar said: [Verbal wrong is more heinous than monetary wrong, because one affects his [the victim's] person, the other [only] his money. Rabbi Samuel bar Nachmani said: For the former restoration is possible, but not for the latter.

were very concerned about the former approach. As Rambam writes (*Hilchos De'os* 1:6), part of our requirements of personal and spiritual development is to become honest people who are sensitive to the needs of others:

> Just as He is called "Gracious," you shall be gracious; Just as He is called "Merciful," you shall be merciful; Just as He is called "Holy," you shall be holy. In a similar manner, the prophets called God by other titles: "Slow to anger," "Abundant in kindness," "Righteous," "Just," "Perfect," "Almighty," "Powerful," and the like. [They did so] to inform us that these are good and just paths. A person is obligated to accustom himself to these paths and [to try to] resemble Him to the extent of his ability.

It is worth considering to what extent Chazal had deep sensitivity to words or actions that create an indignity to the vulnerable or defenseless, and how their model helps us become personalities who are attuned to our elevated status relative to others, even if the other cannot feel the pain of indignity. Take, for example, the following passage (*Berachos* 18a):

> A man should not walk [within four cubits of a] cemetery with *tefillin* on his head or a scroll of the Law in his arm, and recite the *Shema*, and if he does so, he comes under the heading of "He that mocks the poor blasphemes his Maker" (*Mishlei* 17:5).

The Rabbis interpret the phrase *lo'eg la-rash*, "mocks the poor," to be referring to the ultimate poor person, the deceased, who can no longer perform God's commandments. Can there be a greater degradation than to highlight that one is no longer obligated in the *mitzvos*! Obviously, the rotting flesh cannot feel, and the departed soul is not measuring the pedestrian's distance from the grave. Instead, the Rabbis are positing that a person who is sensitive to the suffering of others would want to avoid de facto flaunting behaviors.

What emerges from careful reading of these passages is the deep concern the Sages had for what contemporary researchers call microaggressions. While deliberate, conspicuous, materially impactful aggressions certainly take place in contemporary times, as well as the times of Talmud, they are by no means the only type of injury. For those in minority or vulnerable populations, the daily onslaught of indignities has far reaching, if difficult to measure effects. And as the Torah teaches, Jews should be particularly sensitive to the plight of the marginalized and disenfranchised, as we too were once strangers in a strange land.